*This book is dedicated to
the students of the United States of America
who may one day finish
the March to Freedom.*

Marching to Freedom

The Life of
MARTIN LUTHER KING, JR.

ROBERT M. BLEIWEISS, *Editor*

With Jacqueline L. Harris
and Joseph R. Marfuggi

A SIGNET BOOK

Published by
THE NEW AMERICAN LIBRARY

Library of Congress Catalog Card Number: 68-9356

*Published by arrangement with American Educational
Publications.*

SIGNET TRADEMARK REG. U.S. PAT. OFF. AND FOREIGN COUNTRIES
REGISTERED TRADEMARK—MARCA REGISTRADA
HECHO EN CHICAGO, U.S.A.

*SIGNET BOOKS are published by
The New American Library, Inc.,
1301 Avenue of the Americas, New York, New York 10019*

FIRST PRINTING, NOVEMBER, 1969

PRINTED IN THE UNITED STATES OF AMERICA

Contents

v

Acknowledgments

MANY people at American Education Publications contributed to the creation of this book, but none more than Associate Editors Jacqueline Harris and Joseph Marfuggi, who did virtually all the writing.

Francis Gemme's work on our first three chapters was most helpful. Dr. Robert F. Beauchamp's criticism of our book plan was invaluable, and we are grateful for his continuing role as the editor's conscience. Our thanks to Victor Salvatore, Jr. and C. L. McKelvie for their editorial counsel.

The cover design is by Harry Rich; photographic lay-outs by Alfred Petersen. Our gratitude also to Michael Schinas for gathering photographs and to Jean Russell for her splendid copy editing. Gladys Werner kept our manuscript readable and Ian Stuart was responsible for production coordination.

Our sincere thanks go to Dr. John Maguire, Associate Provost of Wesleyan University in Middletown, Conn., for sharing with us his personal view and understanding of his close friend, Dr. Martin Luther King, Jr.

Robert M. Bleiweiss
June 12, 1968

Chapter I

Memphis: Dynamite On The River

It was Thursday afternoon, April 4, 1968, in Memphis. The Tennessee city was still in the midst of a garbage collectors' strike, but a threat of rioting had faded. Except for the garbage piling up in the streets, it was just another pleasant spring day in Memphis.

At 3:30 that afternoon a tall man with a long, sharp nose asked for a room at Mrs. Bessie Brewer's rooming house. He signed a name—John Willard—and paid Mrs. Brewer $8.50 for a week's rent. She didn't pay much attention to him. "I never really looked too well at his face," she said later, "but there was one thing— he had a silly smile."

The man went upstairs to Room 5. It was perfect. The window in his room faced the Lorraine Motel. He watched. He had plenty of time. From where he sat he could see everyone who went in or out of Room 306 at the Lorraine Motel across the street. He opened a can of beer, sipped it, and waited.

Room 306 was where Dr. Martin Luther King, Jr. was staying while he was in Memphis. The famous civil rights leader was in Memphis to help the garbage collectors win their fight with the city.

The strike began on February 12. The 1,300 garbage collectors asked the city to recognize their union and give them a 60-cent per hour raise. Mayor Henry Loeb, who had taken office on January 1, refused to meet the garbage collectors' demands.

Mayor Loeb feared that if he agreed to the garbage collectors' demands, other city employees would go on strike, too. And if firemen, policemen, and hospital workers demanded more money, the city would have to pay higher wages or be left without protection.

Because the city did not recognize the garbage collectors' union, the mayor claimed the strike was illegal. But the union, Local 1773 of the American Federation of State, County, and Municipal Employees, said it would not go back to work unless one big demand was met. It wanted a dues checkoff system that allows the employer to automatically deduct union dues from each man's paycheck and turn the dues over to the union. The city refused. The dues checkoff would amount to official recognition of the union.

Gradually, the strike became more of a racial struggle than a labor dispute. About 95 percent of the Memphis garbage collectors were Negro. They saw the city's refusal to settle the strike as another form of racial discrimination. Negroes, they claimed, had trouble finding jobs in Memphis. Negroes had to work for less money and were the first to be fired, they said.

Local Negro leaders agreed with the garbage collectors' complaints. "Dignity is the real issue here," a union leader said. "In addition to legal rights, Negroes need economic rights."

Memphis' 280,000 Negroes—nearly 40 percent of the city's population—rallied to the support of the garbage collectors. Negro ministers and civil rights leaders urged the strikers to stay off their jobs until the union's demands were met. Bound together by a newfound toughness, the Negro community united.

An organization called COME, Community on the Move for Equality, was formed by 150 Memphis ministers. The Rev. James Lawson, chairman of the group, explained why he thought the garbage collectors' strike was so important:

"A union for striking workers would take away [the workers'] powerlessness," Reverend Lawson said. "The garbage strike had galvanized our efforts to unite the community . . . I now see the validity of an approach to the problems of poverty that's not based on handouts but on getting more people to insist on decency."

The ministers urged Negroes not to shop in downtown Memphis stores. Among the businesses that Negroes boycotted were a chain of barbecue restaurants and laundries owned by the Mayor's brother.

Memphis Negroes, one leader said, wanted economic black power. "We are going to get more and better jobs from the city and the downtown merchants. And those businesses that are patronized by blacks alone are going to he managed by blacks."

Protesters complained about more than a lack of jobs. Negroes were not equally represented in the city and county governments. And, a protest leader said, Memphis had "no black faces in any high administrative post in the school system."

Another complaint was the city's slowness to carry out urban renewal programs in Negro neighborhoods. White landlords, a civil rights leader charged, influenced city officials to stall tearing down the slum tenements. In the meantime, he claimed, the landlords made big profits on the buildings because they spent no money for maintenance or improvements.

But dignity and decency were at the heart of the Negroes' demands. "We have to win this one," a striker explained. "This is the last chance for many of us to be men." The strikers reflected their desire for dignity in the signs that they carried through the streets. The message was simple—"I Am a Man."

Two days after the boycotts began, nearly 700 protesters took over City Hall. They sat down in the City Council chambers and refused to move. Before they went home, they stayed long enough to eat 110 loaves of bread and stacks of sliced meat.

The city tried to break the strike by hiring new employees. Supervisors drove the garbage trucks, which also carried off-duty policemen for protection. But the city was too short of men to do a good job. Garbage and refuse piled higher. Tensions grew. The strike looked as though it would stretch into weeks.

At night the Negroes met in church halls for rallies and speeches. During the day they marched down Main Street to City Hall. At the end of their marches the strikers faced the multimillion dollar City Hall displaying its bronze seal whose main symbols, a cotton plant and a riverboat, reflect Memphis' history. One Negro marcher called the municipal structure "a white marble arrogance of power."

One day a group of marchers claimed that a police cruiser intentionally bumped the strikers. They rocked the cruiser back and forth, and threatened to turn it over. Policemen quickly used tear gas to break up the march and prevent a riot.

The following week the Negroes staged another sit-in in the council chambers during a meeting. When the strikers refused to leave, the council adjourned. Henry Lux, assistant police chief, warned the crowd: "We do not want any trouble and we do not anticipate any trouble."

The strikers chanted in unison: "We want jail; we want jail." The police moved in and arrested 117 people. Quietly and peacefully, the strikers marched across the street to the police station.

By the fifth week of the strike, businessmen were feeling the effects of the economic boycott. Store owners were selling only about half as many items as normal. A boycott against the two local newspapers cut circulation by 15,000. But the Negroes' message did not get through to the white businessmen. One downtown merchant shrugged his shoulders and remarked: "I don't know what the Negroes are complaining about. I thought we had pretty good relations."

Reverend Lawson was firm. "Who would have thought that the sanitation workers could have galvanized the efforts of the Negro community? The mood of the ministers is that the boycotts should continue. There are other goals to be met, jobs for Negroes, for instance. We don't know exactly what direction it will take, but the white man in Memphis has tried too long to pretend that we don't have racial unrest just like the rest of the country."

Tensions and tempers mounted as the piles of uncollected garbage grew higher. Vandals struck in the middle of the night. Overflowing garbage cans were set on fire while fireman chased down false alarms. Store windows in the downtown district were shattered. Memphis sat on the banks of the Mississippi River like a keg of dynamite over a spreading flame. At any moment, it could explode.

At the invitation of the Memphis ministers, Dr. Martin Luther King, Jr. came to the city to address strikers at a rally.

Dr. King, the Southern minister who was the most famous of all civil rights leaders, had dedicated himself to improving the lives of less fortunate people of the United States. His method was nonviolent protest, but he was as militant as any soldier who ever fought for freedom. He believed in direct action, but without violence. His object was to make every citizen a part of the American dream.

Dr. King led marches and protests all over the country in a nonviolent struggle for better conditions for the Negroes of America. He wanted human rights, better housing and schools, more employment, and greater acceptance and recognition for his people. The Negroes had been exploited as slaves for two hundred years and had been limited to second-class citizenship for the last one hundred. This Dr. King sought to change.

He included other minority groups such as the American Indian and the Mexican American in his movement. He believed that poverty was the greatest blight in the richest country in the world. Poverty also was the largest cause of social and political inequality. Dr. King decided to form what he called a Poor People's March on Washington in the spring of 1968. He hoped the march would arouse the conscience of America to change the condition of the poor.

While preparing for this march in the early spring, Dr. King was asked to come to western Tennessee to help the garbage men of Memphis. He agreed that this was no simple municipal strike. Here were poor men trying to better their lives. Here were men demanding their rights and fighting for dignity.

Dr. King took time out from organizing his Poor People's March to bring his prestige and the power of his organization, the Southern Christian Leadership Conference, to help the Memphis garbage men. The 1,300 strikers warmly welcomed Dr. King's help. City officials and the white population of Memphis opposed his "interference" in what they considered to be just a minor local dispute.

Dr. King spoke to 12,000 listeners. He told the strikers not to get discouraged. "Nothing is gained without sacrifice," he said. He encouraged a one-day, city-wide boycott of work planned for later in the month. He also pledged the financial backing of the Southern Christian Leadership Conference. He said he would return to lead the marchers personally on the day of the work boycott.

The strikers were heartened by this newfound support. The "Yeas" and "Amens" that were the reaction of most of King's black audiences were especially loud when the young minister said that as a result of the boycott: "They will hear you then. The city of Memphis will not be able to function that day." A freak 14-inch snowstorm postponed the day of the boycott until the next Thursday, March 28, 1968.

On March 28, Dr. King led 6,000 marchers down historic Beale Street, where Negro musicians had created a kind of music known as the blues. It's a sad music, filled with haunting memories of troubles and suffering. The blues came back to Beale Street that day.

The march began quietly. The marchers were solemn as they followed Dr. King towards city hall. Then, suddenly, a group of 150 Negro teen-agers broke away from the march. They smashed store windows and lunged at policemen. Before anyone could prevent it, a riot had begun. Stores were looted. Fires were set.

Dr. King's assistants rushed him away from the scene as soon as the rioting began. They were afraid he would be injured if he remained behind.

Memphis police used gas and clubs to break up the riot. Hoping to prevent further trouble, the Governor of Tennessee sent state troopers and 4,000 National Guardsmen to Memphis. By the next morning, 300 people had been arrested. Sixty were injured and a 16-year-old Negro boy was dead. He had been shot by police while he was looting a store.

Dr. King thought that he had failed—that his nonviolent philosophy had been rejected by Memphis Negroes. He seriously considered leaving the city for good. But his supporters at the Southern Christian Leadership Conference convinced him that the violence had been started by a small group of teen-agers. So he agreed to lead another march because, he said, "Nonviolence is on trial in Memphis."

He was right. White critics said Dr. King could no longer control large crowds. The Poor People's March on Washington, they said, should be banned as a safety precaution. Black racists were also glad that Dr. King was in trouble. Nonviolence, they claimed, could never win equality for Negroes.

Dr. King knew that he must prove that his white and black critics were wrong. He knew that he must show America that nonviolent protest was still a powerful and peaceful tactic to bring about constructive change. He ordered his staff to make plans for another Memphis march.

The staff talked to members of the teen-age gang that had rioted during Dr. King's first march. The boys agreed not to start any trouble during the second march.

Before leading the Memphis Negroes in another march, Dr. King scheduled a series of rallies in the city. The first was held April 3. Dr. King spoke to 2,000 spirited followers at the Mason Street Temple. He had attracted the Negro moderates who favored gradual action, as well as the militants who wanted immediate action. A local minister looked out at the unified crowd and whispered to another clergyman, "That's why it's so important that nothing happen to King. Memphis would be smoking right now if it weren't for King." And another minister, speaking to the congregation, said, "King is the man, oh Lord, you have sent to lead us out of Egypt."

Then Dr. King stepped to the pulpit. "It is no longer a question of violence or nonviolence in this day and age," he said. "It is nonviolence or nonexistence."

Above him, a bright neon cross cast its yellow reflection on Dr. King's head and shoulders. He talked about the importance of nonviolence and how it could help the Negro. Then he talked about his own career and death. He told the audience about the many times his life had been threatened. He told them that his flight to Memphis had been delayed while officials searched the airplane for bombs.

"But it really doesn't matter with me now," Dr. King said, "Because I've been to the mountaintop . . . and

I've looked over, and I've seen the promised land." Outside, a heavy spring rain slammed against the metal roof and filled the upper portions of the church with an applause-like hum. And the congregation punctuated Dr. King's speech with spontaneous shouts of "Amen" and "Yes, yes."

He continued, ". . . I may not get there with you, but I want you to know tonight that we as a people will get to the promised land. So I'm happy tonight. I'm not worried about anything. I'm not fearing any man. Mine eyes have seen the glory of the coming of the Lord!"

Deeply moved by Dr. King's words, the congregation filed out of the church into the rainy Memphis night. They were encouraged and uplifted by the speech. They were happy again.

The next day, Thursday, Dr. King planned the steps he and his staff would take in Memphis, beginning with the rally Thursday night. Again and again he emphasized the importance of nonviolence to his assistants, many of whom had been with him for years.

One of those men, Hosea Williams, said later, "Dr. King really preached us a sermon. He said the only hope of redeeming the soul of this nation was through the power of nonviolence . . . and he told us, 'I have conquered the fear of death. . . .' "

While Dr. King and his staff talked and planned in the Lorraine Motel, the man who called himself John Willard sipped beer in his rented room. After about an hour in his room, the man went outside to his car. He came back into the rooming house, carrying the kind of blue satchel that boys take to the gym. Under his other arm he held a high-powered 30.06 pump-action rifle, equipped with a telescopic sight. It was the kind of weapons snipers use.

The man with the "silly smile" climbed the steps to his room. It was almost 5 p.m. It was getting late.

Chapter II

Death: One Minute After Six

Three minutes before six that Thursday afternoon Dr. King stepped onto the balcony outside his motel room. It had been a long day and he wanted some fresh air before he left for dinner and the rally.

Across the street in Mrs. Bessie Brewer's rooming house the man with the sniper's gun had locked himself in a bathroom. He stood in the grimy bathtub and steadied the rifle on the windowsill. He was only 205 feet away from the Lorraine Motel balcony.

Dr. King leaned on the green balcony railing and talked with his driver and friends down below in the motel parking lot. One of the men in the lot was the Rev. Jesse Jackson, one of Dr. King's assistants. He introduced Dr. King to Ben Branch, a musician who was scheduled to play at the rally that night. "Be sure to play 'Precious Lord,'" Dr. King shouted to Branch, "and play it real pretty."

"Take My Hand, Precious Lord" was one of Dr. King's favorite hymns. One of the verses is:

When my way grows drear, precious Lord, linger near;
When my life is almost gone;
Hear my cry, hear my call, hold my hand lest I fall;
Take my hand, precious Lord, lead me home.*

The man standing in Bessie Brewer's bathtub lifted the rifle to his shoulder. He focused the sights on his target, less than a football field away.

The cool, clear air was turning chilly and the driver suggested that Dr. King take a coat to the rally. "Okay, I will," Dr. King said. He started to straighten up, to go back into his room.

---

* *Copyrighted Thomas A. Dorsey, Hill and Range Songs, Inc. 1951. Used by permission.*

The man in the rooming house took a deep breath. It was one minute after six. The index finger of his right hand slowly squeezed against the cold metal trigger. People who did not see Dr. King fall to the concrete balcony floor thought they had heard a firecracker explode.

The rifle blast tore open Dr. King's jaw and neck. The assassin knew he did not need a second shot. He packed his weapon in cardboard, picked up his satchel, and left the rooming house. Outside, he threw his rifle and satchel on the sidewalk. Then he disappeared.

Dr. King's aides and other motel visitors rushed to the second floor balcony. Reverend Jackson held Dr. King's head in his lap until help arrived. A white guest, a member of the Justice Department, ran out of his room with a motel towel to place over the gaping wound. "All I could think of was Kennedy, Kennedy, Kennedy," the man said. "There was so much blood. . . ."

The Rev. Ralph Abernathy, a close personal friend of Dr. King and the man who would succeed him as head of the Southern Christian Leadership Conference, sensed it was too late to save Dr. King. Tears flooded his eyes as he dropped to his knees beside his friend. "Martin," he moaned, "Martin . . . Martin . . ."

Life was quickly draining from Dr. King's body as an ambulance arrived. The dying man was carried into the emergency room at nearby St. Joseph's Hospital at 6:16 p.m. For the next 50 minutes, a team of 12 white doctors made every effort to save Dr. King. But the bullet had severed the spinal cord. Even if Dr. King had survived, he would have been permanently paralyzed from the neck down. One of the doctors said later, "He was essentially dead on arrival."

At 7:05 the civil rights leader was pronounced dead by Memphis coroner Dr. Jerry Francisco. Twenty-five minutes later, one of Dr. King's staff members emerged from the hospital. His eyes were swollen and red from crying as he told reporters, "They have killed Dr. King."

Another staff member said, "He had always lived

with the expectation of assassination but nobody ever expected it to happen."

In Atlanta, Coretta King received a telephone call from Memphis. Dr. King had been wounded, the caller said. Atlanta Mayor Ivan Allen, Jr. was told of the shooting, too, and rushed to the King home to take Mrs. King to the airport. A chartered airliner waited there to take Mrs. King to the side of her wounded husband.

The Mayor's car raced through Atlanta's misty, rainy streets. But at the airport, before Mrs. King got on the plane, someone told Mayor Allen that Dr. King was dead. The Mayor stopped Mrs. King in the airlines terminal and told her the doctors had not been able to save her husband's life. She decided to return home to spend the night with her four children.

Memphis police had sealed off the block around the Lorraine Motel immediately after the shooting. Witnesses said the man who had dropped the rifle outside the rooming house had driven off in a white Mustang car. Roadblocks were set up. The Federal Bureau of Investigation sent agents to Memphis to join the search. But the killer had vanished.

In Washington, President Johnson learned about the shooting while he was discussing the possibility of Vietnam peace talks. Immediately he ordered the Justice Department to investigate the crime. The President was tired. Only four days before he had stunned the world by announcing that he would not seek renomination for another term. He was scheduled to fly to Hawaii for a series of conferences about peace in Vietnam. Then came the message: "Mr. President, Martin Luther King is dead."

President Johnson canceled his trip to Hawaii. He called Mrs. King in Atlanta and expressed his sorrow. Then he wrote a short statement that took him a minute to read on nationwide TV. "America is shocked and saddened by the brutal slaying. . . ." he said. At the end of his brief statement he asked all Americans to remain peaceful as a tribute to the beliefs of Dr. King.

Sen. Robert Kennedy, campaigning for the Democratic presidential nomination, joined the President in his plea for a quiet reaction to Dr. King's death. When

he heard the news, Senator Kennedy went to an Indi-
anapolis ghetto neighborhood. "I have very sad news
for you," he told people in the streets, "Martin Luther
King was shot and killed tonight. . . . For those of
you who are black and are tempted to be filled with
hatred and resentment against the injustice of such an
act—against all white people, I can also feel in my heart
the same kind of feeling—a member of my family was
killed—and he was killed by a white man."

Many other Americans compared the murder of Dr.
King to the assassination of President John F. Kennedy, four and a half years before. European news-
casters referred to Memphis as "another Dallas" and to
Martin Luther King, Jr. as "the black man's President."

Dr. King's death touched off the most widespread
rampage of rioting that America had ever seen. In
Memphis, Washington, Chicago, Detroit, Baltimore,
and a dozen other cities angry Negroes took to the
streets.

Federal troops moved into the nation's capital,
guarding the White House with fixed bayonets. A machine gun nest protected the Capitol.

Washington, where 66 percent of the population is
Negro, had not shared other cities' serious racial dis-
turbances during the preceding four summers. Crowds
began to form as people heard about the murder. They
were angry and upset. Twisted by their emotions, many
people thought the advice of black power leader
Stokely Carmichael made sense.

"Go home and get your guns," Carmichael cried.
"When the white man comes he is coming to kill you.
I don't want any black blood in the street. Go home
and get a gun."

Some people did not need Carmichael to lead them.
As he spoke, teen-agers were already smashing store
windows, looting, and setting fires. The trouble lasted
until dawn. Then it stopped, only to begin again a few
hours later. The looting and burning was worse on Friday. Entire stores were emptied of clothing, food, li-
quor. There was almost a carnival atmosphere in some
areas, as people stopped in the street to try on a new
jacket or a pair of shoes.

Most Negroes did not participate in the rioting and looting. In Chicago, a Negro woman tried to stop a group of looters. "Come out of that store and leave that stuff," she pleaded. "You-all nothing but bums. Ain't we got enough trouble without our neighborhood burning down?"

During the weekend after Dr. King's death, 168 cities and towns felt the pain of some kind of civil disorder. A total of 72,880 Army and National Guard troops had gone on duty across the nation. And 24,000 people had been arrested. Most officials, therefore, were surprised that only 43 people had died during the rioting. It began to appear that, despite the urging of some black power leaders, America would be spared from an all-out racial war.

Police and military troops had learned much from handling riots during the four previous summers. They did not confront rioters unless they had enough force to do so. Arrested suspects were quickly removed from the scene. Curfews proved to be the most effective weapon for control of large areas. Finally, military and civilian officials demonstrated that they did not value property as highly as they did human lives.

In a few cities, officials made personal appearances to head off trouble. Mayor John V. Lindsay of New York and Mayor Carl Stokes of Cleveland made walking tours of tense and troubled areas. Both mayors showed their sorrow over the crime, expressed sympathy to all the Negroes they met, and urged everyone, especially the young, to "cool it." In other cities, young Negro groups with such names as the "Five Percenters," the "Black Panthers," and the "United Community Corps" fanned out through tense neighborhoods urging peace.

In Washington, D.C., a few days after the peak of the rioting, ghetto schoolchildren gave their impressions of the terrifying events.

Some children drew pictures of flaming or gutted buildings and homes. Others drew scenes of storefronts with broken windows and people rushing down the street with armloads of loot. Still other children wrote their impressions of what had happened.

One youngster wrote: ". . . Right now I want to be President. I want to do some shopping. I want to have money. I want to change what's going on. I want to remember Mr. King. I want to forget the rioting."

A second child reflected the burning rage of many Negroes: "The white people killed Martin Luther King. They had no reason. He was helping both white and colored people. I think it was right to destroy all the white folks' stores." A third child said, "Dr. King would feel sad about the riot."

"The saddest thing I saw," said another, "was old ladies getting caught in the fire, and my classmate tear gassed from his home. . . . The nicest thing I saw was white people helping colored people."

Mrs. King held a press conference the weekend between her husband's death and his funeral. "I hope that you who loved and admired him would join us in fulfilling his dream," she said. On Monday, the day before the funeral, she and her three oldest children flew to Memphis. There they led the garbage collectors' march that Dr. King had planned before his death. The mass demonstration was peaceful, just as Dr. King hoped it would be.

Dressed in black, Mrs. King spoke to the solemn marchers. ". . . how many men must die before we can really have a free and true and peaceful society? How long will it take? If we can catch the spirit and the true meaning of this experience, I believe that this nation can be transformed into a society of love, of justice, peace, and brotherhood where all men can really be brothers."

Chapter III

Funeral:
'Free At Last'

April 9, 1968, the day of Dr. King's funeral, was bright and sunny in New York City. As the 49th Street crosstown bus pulled to a stop, a Negro teen-ager wearing jeans and a T-shirt got on. The boy carried a transistor radio. As he paid his fare and moved down the aisle of the bus, the words, "Dr. Martin Luther King will be buried this afternoon," came from his radio. The passengers on the bus fell silent. The subdued voice of a reporter began to describe the scene outside Atlanta's Ebenezer Baptist Church, where the funeral would be held.

At a dress factory on Eighth Avenue, the sewing machines were quiet, as the operators gathered around a small radio. In a Harlem apartment on 116th Street, a Negro family clustered around their television set.

Throughout the country the scenes of silent respect were the same. The closed shops, the flags at half-mast, the peal of bells echoing through the empty streets told the world of America's great sorrow.

Some Americans joined in spirit with those present in the Ebenezer Baptist church by holding their own services. In Illinois, the priests of a Franciscan monastery marched down a highway to a neighboring town where they prayed for the soul of Dr. King and the country he had "tried to love." Five thousand people marched through downtown Minneapolis to Loring Park where they held memorial services. In Chicago, hundreds of people stood in Grant Park on the Lake Michigan shore and bowed their heads in prayer.

Since the assassination on April 4, the days of mourning had been marked by marches and memorial services. After the first shock of the news was absorbed, it was as if people *had* to do something. In small towns and in large cities, black and white Americans walked together along Main Street, U.S.A., in memory of a man whose heart would have warmed at such a sight.

On the Friday after the assassination Americans marched in Selma, Ala., in Madison, Wis., in Austin, Tex., in Birmingham, Ala.

In Washington on that Friday the President, his Cabinet, and other Government officials joined Washingtonians in a memorial service in Washington Cathedral. Only five days earlier Dr. King had given a sermon there. Many of the 4,000 people who attended were in tears. "Forgive us, forgive us, God please forgive us," said Rev. Walter Fauntroy from the pulpit, "Forgive us for our sins that have led to this tragedy." When the service ended, the great cathedral bell began to toll. As the people left the cathedral, a few teen-agers sang softly "We Shall Overcome." Soon all the mourners were singing the civil rights song. The sound filled the great stone cathedral.

On Saturday waterfronts on the East and West coasts were silent and deserted as longshoremen observed a memorial to Dr. King. Ships in port flew their flags at half-mast.

Sunday, April 7, had been designated by President Johnson as a national day of mourning. On that day 25,000 New Yorkers converged on Seventh Avenue and with linked arms wended their silent way through the city. In Columbus, Ohio, thousands of people marched through the fairgrounds to the coliseum where a memorial service was held.

Major events of all kinds were postponed until after the funeral. The American Academy of Motion Picture Arts and Sciences postponed its annual Oscar awards. When the ceremony was finally held on Wednesday evening, much of the customary gaiety was missing. Gregory Peck, the Academy's president, made a short memorial speech to open the ceremonies. When Rod Steiger was named best actor of the year for his performance in "In the Heat of the Night," he made a stirring acceptance speech, ending with the statement "We *shall* overcome."

The opening games of the major league baseball season were postponed so as not to conflict with the day of mourning. Many professional basketball players, in spite of being in the middle of their championship playoffs, went to Atlanta for the funeral. The playoff games were postponed.

Many schools closed on the day of the funeral. Students in Harlem's Booker T. Washington Junior High sat silently at their desks as the news of the school closing came over the public address system. Before they left school for the day, the students talked about who Dr. King was. The teacher wrote their responses on the blackboard . . . "civil rights worker" . . . "won Nobel Prize" . . . "preached nonviolence." One student said, "He believed in equal rights for Negroes." "Just Negroes?" asked the teacher. "For all people," said the entire class. Their homework assignment was to "write a paragraph on why you feel that Dr. King's death was a loss to America."

Colleges across the country closed. In one college as students left a memorial service, some paused to hear a Negro speaker sound a dissonant note outside the chapel. He said, "We don't mourn King. He was an obstacle to the black liberation movement." One student interrupted him with, "All you know is burn, baby, burn. I haven't got any answers—but that isn't it, either."

The world shared America's loss and sadness.

India's Prime Minister Indira Gandhi described Dr. King as "an apostle of peace . . . one of mankind's finest products and a great evangelist of the equality of man." After her speech, the members of the Indian Parliament stood for a minute of respectful silence in honor of Dr. King. The West German Parliament and the Geneva State Assembly of Switzerland also paid this silent tribute to the civil rights leader.

Said Denmark's Foreign Minister Paul Hartling, "Dr. King will not be forgotten. Murder cannot stop his cause."

Pope Paul VI said he prayed that the virtues of justice and fraternal love that Dr. King stood for will come to be respected everywhere.

From Sweden King Gustav VI hoped that "there are people who can complete his work."

Many European newspapers were concerned about the violence in America that had ended the lives of two prominent Americans: "President John Kennedy and Martin Luther King, who were friends and who worked together, were victims of bullets fire by the same assassin—hatred, nonunderstanding," wrote a Madrid newspaper.

"There is something wrong in America, first John Kennedy and now Martin Luther King," said Portugal's *Diario de Lisboa*.

Other newspapers were concerned about the effect of the assassination on the Negro civil rights movement. "If violence takes over, if the black revolution abandons nonviolence, it will be known that the night in Memphis was the beginning," was the opinion of France's *La Croix*.

"One trembles for the future of race relations in the United States. This senseless killing could set things back a decade," warned South Africa's *The World*.

As the messages of sympathy and praise poured into Atlanta and Washington, people were converging on Atlanta.

Dr. King's body lay in state in Atlanta's Spelman College chapel. Long lines of mourners moved past the coffin. As each person moved up to view the body, he found himself face to face with the reality of Dr. King's death. No longer would that baritone voice urging love and justice be heard in the land. Some began to sob and rushed out of the chapel; others bit their lips and turned slowly away.

On Monday night the body was brought to Ebenezer Baptist Church to lie before the altar. There in the simple church where Dr. King and his father had preached, the funeral would be held. Still, the people came "to say good-by to Martin." Through the night they filed through the dimly lit church. These were the ordinary black people, men in their worn Sunday suits, ladies in their black "mournin'" dresses, teen-agers wearing jackets that said "Black Is Beautiful"—and white people, their clothes often rumpled from traveling.

As they moved past the coffin and out into the soft

Atlanta night, they gathered in groups near the entrance to the church. By 5 a.m., as the first rays of sunlight streamed through the dogwood blossoms, hundreds were keeping the silent watch. By 10:30 a.m.
50,000 people stood outside the church—marines in
crisp tan uniforms, postal workers, slim white co-eds,
Negro maids, white priests. Most of those people were
not admitted into the church, which could seat only
800. The space inside the church was reserved for the
family, old friends, members of the Ebenezer congregation, and many of the dignitaries who attended.

Inside the church, fragrant with the smell of flowers,
the black-robed choir filed into their places at the front
of the church. High above the choir a stained-glass window depicting a kneeling Christ sent filtered sunlight
into the church. On the closed coffin in front of the
pulpit was a cross made of white chrysanthemums and
lilies. Flanking the coffin were more flowers. Poking
through the draperies behind the choir, a television
lens could be seen carrying the service to an estimated
120 million viewers throughout the land.

Among the dignitaries in the church were government people such as Vice-President Hubert H. Humphrey; Senators Robert F. and Edward M. Kennedy;
Governor Nelson Rockefeller; Senator Eugene Mc-
Carthy; Carl Stokes, the Negro Mayor of Cleveland;
and John V. Lindsay, Mayor of New York City.

Among the diplomats were Ambassador to the
United Nations Arthur J. Goldberg; the Ambassador
from Morocco to the U.N.; the Ambassador to the
U.N. from Guinea; and Dr. Ralph J. Bunche, who represented the Secretary General of the U.N., U Thant.
Basketball stars Wilt Chamberlain of the Philadelphia
76ers and Bill Russell of the Boston Celtics, former
heavyweight boxing champion Floyd Patterson, and
baseball great Jackie Robinson were there.

Entertainment stars present included Harry Belafonte, Marlon Brando, Godfrey Cambridge, Bill Cosby,
Robert Culp, Ossie Davis, Sammy Davis, Jr., Ben Gaz-
zara, Mahalia Jackson, and Diana Ross and the Su-
premes. Prominent churchmen present were Arch-
bishop John F. Dearden of Detroit and Rabbi Harold

Gordon, Executive Director of the New York Board of Rabbis. Mrs. John F. Kennedy; former Vice-President Richard M. Nixon; Whitney M. Young, Director of the Urban League; and Andrew Heiskell, Chairman of the Board of Time, Inc., were also there.

Leading the family into the church, Reverend Abernathy intoned, "I am the resurrection and the life; he that believeth in me, though he were dead, yet shall he live."

The ceremonies included eulogies by Dr. King's fellow ministers. Dr. Harold de Wolf, a Boston University professor who had taught Dr. King, also spoke. The choir sang some of Dr. King's favorite hymns, "Softly and Tenderly," "Where He Leads Me," and "I Shall Not Have Died in Vain."

Reverend Abernathy began his eulogy by announcing that he had fasted since the night Dr. King was killed. The fast, he said, was a preparation for his new position as leader of the Southern Christian Leadership Conference.

A tape recording of one of Dr. King's sermons was played in which he talked about his own death and funeral. "I don't want a long eulogy . . . just say that I tried to love somebody." As the words echoed through the old church, awed silence was broken only by the muffled sounds of people weeping. One elderly woman cried out, "We gonna see him no more."

Outside the church two mules were being hitched to a weathered green farm wagon. The wagon and the mules, symbols of the poverty Dr. King was trying to wipe out, would carry the body along the procession route to Morehouse College, the small Negro college from which Dr. King had graduated.

With Reverend Abernathy leading the procession, the gleaming mahogany coffin was carried out of the church and placed on the wagon.

As the mules began the 4-mile journey across town to the second service, they were followed by 150,000 marchers. White and black, governor and farmer, they moved down Auburn Avenue where Dr. King had been born. Past the Georgia statehouse, they walked. Inside his heavily guarded office Gov. Lester Maddox, a segregationist, watched the procession on TV while his aides peered through the venetian blinds. Only because of pressure by his Secretary of State had he allowed the flag to be flown at half-mast over the capitol building.

The procession moved down Mitchell Street toward Morehouse. As the marchers passed over the Hunter Street viaduct into the Negro west side, they began to sing, "This Little Light of Mine."

As the mules approached the archway leading into the college campus, the dense crowds of people on both sides of the street pushed forward. For an instant the mules stopped, their eyes rolled back, their ears flattened against the sides of their heads. But then they were calm and moved quietly to the gate.

It was 3 p.m. when the hymns and eulogies began at Morehouse. The crowd that assembled at the college was huge. It was impossible to see anything from the outskirts. The crush near the podium was such that people were asked several times to move back. The ceremonies at Morehouse involved several hours of hymns and eulogies. Much of the planned program was omitted when it was realized that several more hours might be needed.

Dr. King's widow, Coretta, moved calmly through all of this. An unassuming and soft-spoken woman, she had strongly supported her husband in his work. Few Americans, however, were aware of her, since much of what she did was in the background. The assassination thrust her squarely into the public eye. Her serenity and self-containment gave strength to everyone.

Coretta King had had a long time to prepare for this ordeal. From the beginning of her husband's work, they both knew that it might end this way at any moment and without warning. After it happened, she told 12-year-old Yolanda (Yoki) first. Yoki said, "You're such a brave lady. . . . I'm going to help you. I'm not going to cry." Then they fell into each other's arms and sobbed. "I think I'm scared," said 10-year-old Martin Luther III. The children drew strength from their mother. They, too, went through the long days that followed their father's death with dignity and poise.

On the day of the funeral, five days after the assassination, Mrs. King was still composed. That morning she received a visit from Mrs. John F. Kennedy. The two widows spoke for five minutes. Then the family left the house to go through the long hours of the funeral and their last march with Dr. King.

As the ceremonies at Morehouse ended, the marchers rallied for one final, swaying chorus of "We Shall Overcome." After that, all that remained was to remove Dr. King's body to the cemetery for burial.

Martin Luther King, Jr. was buried at South View, a cemetery established by some of Atlanta's black people who were tired of having to use the back gate of the city cemetery when they wished to bury one of their dead. The coffin was placed to rest. Into the headstone was carved the final phrase of Dr. King's famous "I Have a Dream" speech: "Free at last, free at last, thank God almighty, I'm free at last."

After the funeral some Americans turned from the eulogies and words of praise to actions that would show that they believed in what Dr. King had died for. The President's recent riot commission report pointed the way. This book describes in detail the commission's findings about the conditions under which America's black urban poor live. It tells how the ghettos were created and what keeps them in existence.

Boston University announced ten new scholarships for underprivileged students from distressed areas. Colorado State University started a Martin Luther King graduate scholarship fund. "The aim of the fund is to produce a thousand Luther Kings for the one we lost," said a sociology professor at the college.

In Quincy, Mass., an all-white high school petitioned that Negro students be bussed to their school.

The Scovill Manufacturing Company in Waterbury, Conn., announced that it would start a special fund to aid destitute Negro families in the area.

Levitt and Sons, the firm that built the Levittown housing communities, announced that henceforth it would not permit segregation or discrimination in any Levitt development.

In Congress, too, the assassination of the black leader

had some impact. After President Johnson made his first public statement reacting to the murder, it was believed that he would make a personal appeal to the legislators to pass a pending civil rights bill. It became evident that many congressmen felt that such an address would put extraordinary pressure upon them from the President. Congress might have reacted unfavorably to such an action on the part of the nation's Chief Executive, so no speech was made. The bill had been passed by the Senate.

Fair and open housing for Americans regardless of their race would be guaranteed by this proposed legislation. It also contained sections guaranteeing protection of civil rights workers and for aiding American Indians. The bill was delayed in the House of Representatives for several days. For a time it seemed that the bill would not pass. Then, on April 10, the House sensed the mood of the country and passed the 1968 Civil Rights Act by a vote of 250-171.

The bill's passage was accompanied by much relief and rejoicing. Civil rights leaders cautioned against too much celebration. They pointed out that many, but not all, of the problems of the ghetto poor would be solved by this new law. They were concerned that too many Americans might mistakenly believe that the country had truly reached Dr. King's goals.

It rained the day after the burial in South View Cemetery. Flower petals floated in puddles of water. After the rain ended, seven white women wearing slacks and cotton dresses visited the grave site. They stood in silence and inspected the inscription on the tomb. Then one of the women said, "It was kind of like history. I expect he was a good man regardless of the color of his skin." The women straightened some of the wreaths and went away.

They left him there, resting on a small hillside overlooking the city of his birth.

Chapter IV

Birth:
A Shared Burden

The Rev. Michael Luther King walked the floor in the gray and white house on Auburn Avenue in Atlanta, Ga. Upstairs, his wife was giving birth to their second child. The young minister's brow was wrinkled with concern, and he did not seem to notice the activity around him. Women bustled about, carrying blankets and towels. Great pots of water boiled on the stove. Whispered conferences were held at the front door.

Reverend King's wife, Alberta, went through more than 24 hours of pain before she finally gave birth to a son on January 15, 1929. The baby did not move, did not breathe. Was he dead? The doctor gave the baby's bottom a few brisk slaps. There was a weak cry and then a stronger one. Life had begun for Michael Luther King, Jr.

The baby was born into comfort and security, a world of clean sheets and nourishing food. In the slums of Atlanta, many tiny babies did not have such advantages. But this baby immediately shared a burden with many of those babies in the slums. He was a Negro. In 1929 law and custom in Atlanta, in the state of Georgia, in the United States of America, placed the Negro automatically in an inferior position to white people. The roots of the system that declared a healthy baby inferior at birth because of skin color went back 300 years.

King's ancestors came from Africa. Some came voluntarily to make their way in the new country. Some came as slaves, torn from their native villages and sold like cattle to landowners. They were needed in the New World of the mid-18th century that was suddenly producing huge crops of rice, tobacco, and cotton. Slave labor was a cheap answer to this great need for field hands.

To justify the buying and selling of human beings, the rulers of Great Britain's colonies in the Western Hemisphere passed laws depriving slaves of their human rights. If a slave were not really human then it was not wrong to separate a family forever by selling the mother, father, or children. Even when the family was kept together, the slave owner, not the father, was the head of the family. Healthy Negro women were bred like cattle to produce more slaves. A Negro baby sold for as much as $200. This was a great deal of money then, and slave selling was a very profitable business.

It was a crime to teach slaves to read or to give them a Bible. Since the laws said that slaves were personal property and not really people, they could be, and were, treated like horses or dogs.

By 1807 a "half slave and half free" United States was beginning to feel annoying pangs of conscience. A national law was passed which forbade bringing more slaves into the country. Slavery began to die out in the North. But the South, which was more dependent on agriculture than the North, clung to the cheap labor source. Slavery became a bitter issue between North and South. In February 1861, ten southern states broke away from the rest of the country.

On April 12, 1861, Southern cannonballs crashed against the walls of Fort Sumter, S.C. North and South went to war. Near the end of the war, President Abraham Lincoln freed the slaves by an executive order known as the Emancipation Proclamation. The Northern victory in 1865 doomed slavery forever in America. The 13th, 14th, and 15th amendments to the Constitution officially abolished slavery and gave the ex-slaves all the rights of citizens, including the right to vote.

For a while it looked as if Negroes had been given instant equality. They crowded the voting places and elected several Negro senators and mayors, and even a Negro governor. Negro children went to school. Negro mothers began to dream the all-American dream—that someday their son might be President of the United States.

It did not last long.

Although slavery had been abolished, pro-slavery groups were determined to keep the Negro as nearly inferior as he had been when he was a slave. Terrorist organizations such as the Ku Klux Klan, Mother's Little Helpers, and the Baseball Club of the First Baptist Church were organized. Negro elected officials were murdered, sometimes in broad daylight, while many people stood by and watched. Negro voters were terrorized. During the years 1873-80, approximately 170 Negroes were murdered each year. Little or no effort was made to search out and punish the murderers.

By law, myth, and custom those white people in favor of slavery did everything possible to keep the Negro from enjoying the opportunities and privileges available to the white man. Today many white people still believe that Negroes ought to be treated as inferiors.

In the South segregation laws were passed after the Civil War that prevented Negroes from being treated in white hospitals. Negroes could not attend white schools, could not play in white parks, had to ride in the back of buses and trains, could not use restrooms nor drink from fountains used by whites. There were even laws in some states that said that Negroes and whites could not play checkers or go fishing together. One law said that Negro and white millworkers could not look out of the same window. Those Negroes who broke these laws often were beaten or murdered by angry lynch mobs.

Negroes did not have the chance to vote to change these laws, nor even to object to them. Often the polling places would be concealed so that Negroes could not find them. The threat of brute force made sure they did not try to vote. Any Negro who did manage to vote faced loss of his job, and even a lynch mob.

In 1896 the Supreme Court said that segregation laws did not violate the 14th Amendment, so long as Negro rest rooms, drinking fountains, schools, hospitals, and parks were as good as the ones for whites. But this was not always so. The Negro school might be a wooden shack with benches and only a few books, while the white children attended a large well-equipped school. The water fountain marked "white" was usually a gleaming refrigerated cooler while the one marked "colored" might be just a water tap.

Supreme Court Justice John M. Harlan who voted against the segregation laws in 1896 said, "What can more certainly arouse race hate than state enactments which . . . proceed on the ground that colored citizens are so inferior and degraded that they cannot be allowed to sit in public coaches occupied by white citizens? That, as all will admit, is the real meaning of such [laws]."

In the North there were no laws that enforced segregation. But there were the little lies that had the same effect. "I'm sorry but you must have a reservation." "You must be a member to swim here." "No opening." "No vacancy." "Restricted." In restaurants there were the eggshells sprinkled on top of scrambled eggs served to the unwanted Negro customer. In department stores Negroes had to buy hats, dresses, suits, or shoes without trying them on. These and many other unkind acts and words left deep, painful scars.

Then there were the wild and distorted myths—passed from parent to child—"Negroes have tails; they carry disease; their brains are smaller; they are more animal than human; they are savages; they are dirty, smelly, and lazy."

A famous writer, H. L. Mencken, once wrote, "The educated Negro of today is a failure, not because he meets [difficulties] in life, but because he is a Negro. His brain is not fitted for the higher forms of mental effort; his ideals remain those of a clown."

Terrorism, Southern laws, Northern lies, and myths were all meant to keep the Negro as nearly inferior as he was while enslaved.

Negroes reacted to their situation in different ways.

Some took all the attacks on their human dignity without a word of protest. Some took their troubles to their church. There the ministers told them to forgive their enemies. Spirituals such as "Nobody Knows the Trouble I've Seen" gave them a way to express their sorrow. The words gave them the feeling that God was watching over them and would help them.

Other Negroes could not ignore the voice inside them that said, "You are as good as any other man." They formed organizations such as the National Association for the Advancement of Colored People (NAACP), which fought segregation laws in the courts. Others fought the system by violating unjust laws until their death—often at the hands of white men who passed out swift and violent punishment.

Some Negroes began to believe that they actually were inferior and they hated themselves and other Negroes for it. Such a man was James Albert King, the father of Michael King, Sr. He showed this hatred by drinking and by beating his wife. Drinking helped him forget the hopeless life he led.

Jim King was a sharecropper on a farm in Stockbridge, Ga., a small town about 20 miles from Atlanta. He farmed another man's land and paid him for its use by giving him half of the profits from the harvested crop. The landowner provided him with land, a house, seed, fertilizer, and sometimes food. Because Jim King could neither read nor write, the landowner kept the accounts. Most freed slaves turned to sharecropping after the Civil War. They had no property nor money and their skills were chiefly in the area of farming or other field work. Early in his life Jim dreamed of owning a farm someday. But he could never seem to make a profit. Instead, he usually ended the year by owing huge amounts of money to the store.

Jim and his wife, Delia, had ten children. Michael Luther King was the second child and the oldest son. When he was born, his father wanted to call him Martin and his mother wanted to call him Michael. As long as his mother lived, he was Michael. It was not until 1934 that Michael had his name legally changed to Martin. Michael King became Martin Luther King, Sr.

Although Michael went to school only three months out of the year, he was a bright and ambitious young man. He made spending money for himself and extra money for his family by raising and selling hogs. He managed to save enough to buy a colt. It was the first horse or mule that anyone in his family had ever owned.

Michael often wondered why his father didn't own anything. He got the answer one day when he went with his father to settle accounts with the landowner. His father reported the number of bales of cotton he was turning in. After the landowner checked his books, he said that Jim's debts balanced exactly with his profits. Then Michael remembered that there were seven and a half bags of cottonseed out in the wagon. "Papa, what about the cottonseed outside?" He knew that the cottonseed was worth about a thousand dollars to his father. The "uppity" young boy enraged the landlord who did not like the idea of Jim's getting a profit. "What you got your mouth in it for?" He lifted his foot to kick the boy, but Jim promised that he would discipline his son for daring to speak up for his father.

Michael's mother washed and ironed for a white woman who lived in a brick house. When he was a small boy, he often went to visit his mother while she worked. Once the woman's children invited him in for lunch. But their mother said, "Come around to the back door." She then shut the front door in his face. At the half-opened back door, he was handed a sandwich. In the kitchen he could see his mother ironing the white people's clothes. He threw the sandwich away and ran all the way home thinking, "Someday I'm going to have a brick house and my brick house will be the finest of all." The brick house became a symbol of achievement to him. It was the one thing that would make him as good as the white man.

By the time he was 16, Michael could see that there was no future for him in Stockbridge. He did not want to work all his life and have nothing to show for it as his father had. He was sure that if he went to Atlanta and got a job that someday he would have his brick house.

And so the country boy, unskilled and uneducated, arrived in the big city. He found a job as a mechanic's helper and went to school at night. By the time he was 25 he had earned a high school diploma. He joined a church and felt an attraction to stand in the pulpit and say eloquent and uplifting words. Soon he was the pastor of two small churches. In the meantime he had en-

rolled as a freshman at Morehouse College in Atlanta.
In 1926 he married Alberta Williams, the daughter of
Rev. A. D. Williams, a leading Negro minister. The Reverend Williams was the pastor of the Ebenezer Baptist
Church.

Reverend Williams was a member of a Negro citizens
group that forced the city to build a Negro high school
and a YMCA branch for the Negro community. When
the Atlanta newspaper, *The Georgian,* called the Negro
citizens' group "dirty and ignorant," Reverend Williams
organized a boycott of the paper. As many as 6,000 Negroes dropped the paper in one day. The newspaper
went bankrupt. When Reverend Williams died in 1931,
his son-in-law became pastor of Ebenezer Baptist
Church.

Rev. Martin Luther King, Sr. became a leader of
those Negroes who opposed the indignities of segregation in Atlanta. He was a power in the local NAACP
branch and the Atlanta Negro Voters League. He refused to ride the segregated buses. He led a battle to obtain equal pay for Negro teachers. He managed to get
the elevators in the courthouse integrated. Many times
he received threatening letters from the Ku Klux Klan.
Often when the phone rang in the house on Auburn
Avenue, the person at the other end spat forth threats
and insults.

Reverend King, Sr. finally moved into his brick
house with his family when Martin, Jr. was 13. In
reaching for that goal he had managed to achieve far
more. He had become an important leader of his people, and he created a stable, loving home in which
young Martin, Jr. was to grow and prepare for his
participation in future world-shaking events.

Chapter V

Boyhood:
Shadow Of Hate

Martin Luther King, Jr. stood before delegates to a Baptist convention. He was small and thin and his ears were very large. On his face was the angelic look that only a four-year-old boy soprano can have.

He took a deep breath and began to sing "I Want To Be More and More Like Jesus." It was his favorite song and he sang with gusto. At the end of each phrase of the song, a few people would sing out "Amen." It was Martin's first realization that people could be moved by his words and he found it very exciting.

On Sunday mornings after that he watched his father in the pulpit. People's imaginations were captured by the moving sermons of Reverend King. Young Martin longed to move people the same way. Words, ideas, and their effect on people became the great influence in his life. Words could make people change their minds, could change their lives. Words were powerful. "Someday," the boy said to his mother, "someday, you just wait and see, I'm going to get me some big words."

At the age of five, Martin demanded that he be allowed to go to school with his older sister who was in the first grade. His age was "pushed up" a year and he was enrolled in his sister's class. Unfortunately Martin gave away his secret when he treated his class to a vivid description of his recent fifth birthday party. That ended his school career for a time. But it wasn't long before he was a legally enrolled first grader.

Martin was six when he first encountered the problem that would make "getting some big words" very important.

Among his playmates were the two sons of a white grocery store owner. The day came when the boys' mother said that they could not play with Martin anymore. Martin did not understand the excuses that were offered to him. Finally the woman blurted out, "They're getting too old to play with niggers." Martin was bewildered. What did it mean? The problem seemed to be that he wasn't as good as the white boys. He couldn't understand. He rushed home to ask his mother.

With a sigh, his mother sat down to tell her six-year-old son about the fears and cruelties of some people. His mother ended her explanation of slavery and segregation by saying, "Don't let this thing make you feel you are not as good as white people. You are as good as anyone else and don't you forget it."

The shadow of racial hatred and discrimination had fallen across young Martin's life. It was a shadow that would lengthen and darken as he grew to manhood. But for the time being it remained just a shadow and did not threaten the comfortable and secure life he led.

The Kings lived at the time in a rambling, 12-room frame house on Auburn Avenue. Auburn Avenue started at the foot of Atlanta's famous Peachtree Street, and it was *the* street in the Negro section of Atlanta. The house belonged to Mrs. King's parents, Rev. and Mrs. A. D. Williams. Reverend and Mrs. King, Sr. moved in temporarily when they were newlyweds. There was plenty of room in the house and the arrangement seemed so agreeable to all that the young couple stayed on. The neighborhood was a combination of substantial homes like the Kings' and shacks and double tenements.

Despite the Great Depression of the early 1930's, there was always meat on the table in the house on Auburn Avenue. There were Sunday clothes and allowances and bicycles for the children.

In the King household father's word was final. All was discipline, order, and affection. Martin, his older sister Willie Christine, and his younger brother Alfred Daniel learned to respect hard work, honesty, thrift, order, and courtesy. They were taught that education was the key to a useful life and that the church was the key to a moral life. The children were required to memorize Bible verses and to recite them at the dinner table. Days began and ended with family prayer.

Reverend King often had the children administer

punishment to each other. In this way he hoped to make them realize that punishment for breaking a rule was not personal, although he decided on the number of blows their little bottoms should receive. Martin could never bring himself to hit his sister and he did not care much for hitting his brother. But he willingly accepted punishment from them. When he was being punished, he'd stand silently with his fists clenched. The tears would flow but he never made a sound. The stubborn, quiet-spoken little boy seemed to have a will of steel.

Once when his brother was teasing their sister Chris, Martin first pleaded then demanded that he stop. But A.D., as he was called in the family, continued until Chris was in tears. Martin could stand it no longer. He picked up the phone and hit A.D. over the head with it. The blow knocked A.D. unconscious. Cold water brought him to. A.D. gave second thought to teasing Martin or Chris after that.

Martin was growing into a strong and sturdy competitor. He first practiced basketball shots by bouncing balls against the side of the house. He and his buddies then constructed a basketball court in the King backyard. The open field behind the house became their baseball diamond. Martin was a determined player in all games. His friends often thought that he was fighting instead of playing.

Once when A.D. was at bat he accidentally hit Martin, the catcher, with the bat. Although the blow sent him sprawling, Martin was quick to jump up to protest that A.D. was "out" for missing the third strike.

Martin often won disputes by his persuasive arguments. But sometimes the winner could be determined only after a tussle on the lawn. One time, though, Martin was beaten and kicked down some steps by Black Billy, the school bully. Strangely, he did not raise a hand to defend himself. When A.D. heard about the incident, he was determined to go after Black Billy and avenge the King name. But Martin talked him out of it. Why did the brave wrestler on the lawn let a bully push him around? Was he scared? Maybe. Perhaps he was puzzled by the senselessness of Black Billy's attack. Or did he see the difference between settling a boyish argument on the grass and fighting back after an un-provoked attack. The fact is that he chose not to meet an injustice with another injustice, and he insisted that his brother make the same choice. This was his first use of the nonviolence for which he was to become famous during his lifetime.

From the time he was able to reach the pedals, Mar-tin had a bike. He went everywhere on it. Once after a slight brush with a truck, the rear tire of his bike was flattened. Martin kept pedaling and rode home on the rim.

Often when Martin's mother could not find him she called Alonzo Johnson's house. Alonzo's mother was a very good cook and Martin especially liked her black-eyed peas and collard greens. He and Alonzo built model airplanes and kites together and tried out their creations in the field behind Martin's house. Some-times they tried out their arms by chunking rocks—not at each other, not at first that is. Sometimes the test of skill would become a game of throwing and ducking.

At the age of seven, Martin thought he would start a business. He decided to go into the soft drink indus-try. With A.D. and Chris as partners and with the fi-nancial support of his father, he set up a stand on the front lawn. Customers came and the soft drink business managed to pay off all its debts. There were no profits because the owners helped themselves too often to their product.

When he was eight years old, the shadow that he did not really understand fell across his life again. His fa-ther had taken him to Five Points, a shopping district in Atlanta, to buy a new pair of shoes. The two took seats in the front of the store. The white clerk said to them, "If you'll take seats in the back of the store, I'll wait on you."

"Nothing wrong with these seats," said Reverend King.

"But I can't wait on you here," said the clerk.

"We'll either buy shoes, sitting right here, or we won't buy any of your shoes at all," said Reverend King.

With that he took Martin's hand and stalked out of the store. As they went out onto the sidewalk, Reverend King said, "I don't care how long I have to live with this system, I am never going to accept it. I'll oppose it until the day I die."

Martin could see that his father was angry and for the second time Martin felt hurt by the shadow. His father's word was law in the King household and at Ebenezer Baptist Church. But the shadow seemed to be too much for even his father to conquer. There were times later when Martin feared he would never get a new pair of shoes. His father always refused to buy shoes unless they were allowed to try them on in the front row of seats in the store.

Southern white people often called Negro men by their first name, or simply "boy" if they didn't know the name. Martin's father was always "straightening the white folks out." He insisted on courtesy in public places. Once when Martin was in the car with his father, a police officer stopped the car. Walking over to the car, the officer said, "Boy, what d'ya mean running the stop sign?"

"I'm Reverend King," said Martin's father. Then pointing to his son, he said, "That's a boy, there. Speak up, Son. Tell the officer your name."

The policeman was so flustered that he almost forgot to write out the ticket.

Following grade school, Martin attended Laboratory High School. Laboratory High was a progressive school, rated nationally as superior. Martin was a B-plus student. He and Chris studied together. She tutored him in spelling while he tutored her in mathematics. After Martin had been at Laboratory High for two years, the school was discontinued. He transferred to Booker T. Washington High.

Martin's grandmother, Mrs. Williams, died when he was 13. He had been her special favorite. Mrs. Williams was about to speak at a Baptist Women's Day program when she suffered a heart attack. She was rushed to a hospital, but she died on the way. Martin was watching a big parade at the time. When he heard the news, he hurried home. He found his whole family in tears. It was the first time that the death of a loved one had touched his life. He had been just a baby when Reverend Williams, his grandfather, had died. To think that he had sneaked away from the house to watch a parade while his grandmother was dying was too much for the sensitive boy. He became hysterical, ran upstairs, and threw himself out of a window. He was stunned, but not seriously hurt by the fall.

Soon after Mrs. Williams' death the family began to look around for another house. The neighborhood was becoming more commercial and more run-down. Besides, the old house painfully reminded everyone of Mrs. Williams. They found another house three blocks away on Boulevard. It was a yellow brick house and it sat on a high terrace. Reverend King, Sr. finally had his brick house.

Martin became a teen-ager in the new house. He tried cigarettes behind the fence. Things he never bothered about were becoming very important. Before he rushed off to school in the morning, he took a quick glance at himself in the mirror. Then he would check the shine on his shoes. Tweed suits became his trademark. His friends, "Rooster" Cash, "Shag" Roberts, "Sack" Jones, and "Mole" Everett gave him the nickname "Tweed." Martin also began to take more than passing notice of Chris's girl friends.

His respect for the power of words continued to grow. Public speaking was one of his favorite subjects in school. He practiced his speeches in front of the mirror. Shortly before he finished high school, he won an Elks oratorical contest. He spoke on the subject of "The Negro and the Constitution."

Once at a high school dance, a group of boys crashed the dance. The schoolboys faced the newcomers. A riot seemed inevitable. Martin came forward, controlled his natural fear, and managed to talk the gate-crashers into leaving.

He was "getting his big words." He was also meeting the disturbing shadow of racial discrimination and segregation more and more frequently.

He felt the ugly shadow again while returning from a speech contest. He, a teacher, and his fellow Negro students took seats on a bus. Some white passengers got on later but could not find seats. The bus driver ordered the students to give their seats to the white passengers. Martin and the other students would not move. The bus driver became furious and called the students vile names. He became so insulting and enraged that the teacher feared for the safety of the students in her charge. She advised the students to give up their seats. They did, grumbling. They stood in the aisle the whole 90 minutes back to Atlanta. Martin had never been so angry before. He came very close to hating white people that night.

Shortly after that Martin went to a downtown movie in Atlanta. He was forced to enter the theater through the back door. The section Negroes were forced to sit in was so filthy that he could not enjoy the picture. He never went again.

During the summer of 1944 Martin made his first trip north. He took a train to Connecticut to pick tobacco during the school vacation. There were no separate rest rooms or waiting rooms. He did not feel the atmosphere of fear and worry that seemed to hang over the South. It was a whole new experience for Martin. He saw that there could be a better way for people to live together.

Day after day he and his friends picked tobacco in the hot sun. On the weekends they went into Hartford. There they enjoyed the new freedom of entering restaurants, theaters, and other public places. Hatred existed in Hartford as in Atlanta. But it was expressed in different ways up North. Martin learned that he could be hurt and insulted because of his race no matter where he was. He began to see that the shadow could take many forms and did not cast its dark presence only over the South.

The summer passed and the time came for Martin to return to Atlanta. Sitting on the "colored" side of the curtain in the dining car, he felt as if a curtain had been dropped down on his whole life.

Now he saw the shadow for what it was. It was a kind of theft. By declaring him inferior, white people were attempting to steal his feeling of worth and add it to their own. The result of this realization on Martin was fear. He feared the whites because he never knew what insult he might have to endure next. Whites feared him and other Negroes because they never knew when a Negro might lash out at the injustice.

Before, the shadow had been something that puzzled him or that hurt his feelings. Now he was growing older and moving around in the world. He saw with frightening clearness that the shadow could do him real harm, harm that might damage him forever.

The shadow could make him feel worthless, if he let it. His parents had taught him that a moral life was the key to worth. He remembered his mother's advice, "You are as good as anyone else and don't you forget it."

From his parents Martin had learned to be physically and mentally tough. The shadow, no matter how unjust it was, would not make him hate nor forget that he was as good as anyone. But at the same time, he felt that the injustice had to be wiped out. Martin could see that this would be something he would work for during his life.

Following his return from Hartford in 1944, he took college entrance examinations. The results of the examinations let him skip the twelfth grade. He had already skipped the ninth grade. At the age of 15 he was ready for college. He was a sensitive but strong willed young man with a respect for the power of words. Most important, he could see that life had a specific mission in store for him.

Chapter VI

College:
Message Of Love

It was September 1944. Martin Luther King, Jr. entered Sale Hall chapel on the campus of Morehouse College in Atlanta, Ga. The chapel was a small auditorium with about 550 seats. The only decoration on the walls was a picture of the President of the college, Dr. Benjamin Mays.

Along with other freshmen, Martin took his seat. There was little conversation as the 206 freshmen looked each other over. Soon they would be welcomed into college life at Morehouse by the President and other college officials.

The college officials filed onto the speakers' platform. All eyes turned automatically to Dr. Mays. He was the sort of man whose appearance and manner commanded attention the minute he walked into a room. He was a very tall, dark man, with steel-gray hair. Dr. Mays welcomed the new students and told them what was required of them as Morehouse men. They were expected to believe in themselves and to succeed in life, he said. They were expected to be leaders with determination and daring. A Morehouse man cannot fail, he said.

This was the first of many chapel convocations that Martin would attend. Dr. Mays, an eloquent speaker, a minister, a college President, became an inspiration to him.

After the program in the chapel, the students began several days of psychological testing, physical examinations, and orientation. Student guides took them on a tour of the campus. The Morehouse College campus was small. It was located in what was called the university center, which included the campuses of four other Negro colleges. The entrance to the campus was framed by a wide brick archway. The buildings were old and many were covered with ivy vines. A bell tower high atop one of the dormitories could be seen throughout Atlanta. Martin located the science building, the President's house, the gym, and other buildings he would have to find when classes started.

In a few days the upperclassmen arrived. They immediately began a week-long initiation for the new students. It was the kind of good-natured teasing customary in many colleges. Martin and the other freshmen were forced to wear maroon caps. Maroon and white were the school colors. The upperclassmen insisted on respect from the lowly freshmen.

"Call us mister," they said.

Any freshman who could not recite all the words to the Morehouse hymn might have a wide part shaved down the center of his head. Or he might be thrown into a cold shower with all his clothes on. A freshman might be asked to give a speech on what a Morehouse man was. "I don't know," said one desperate freshman, "but I know I want to be one."

Martin signed up as a sociology major and began his studies. He found the atmosphere in his classes very exciting. For the first time he actually participated in a discussion on racial injustice. Never before had he heard it said in a classroom that segregation was wrong and should be abolished. "Nobody here is afraid," he thought.

Morehouse College is a private college. This meant that it did not depend for its funds on the state of Georgia or the city of Atlanta. Independence from Southern government money meant that racial injustice could be called just that, without the fear that funds needed for operating the college would be cut. The schools Martin had attended earlier received state funds; this was one of the reasons teachers did not feel free to discuss segregation in class.

Martin was an honor student. He sang in the glee club, joined the campus chapters of the Young Men's Christian Association and the National Association for the Advancement of Colored People. He was a member of the student-faculty discipline committee. He pursued his love for the power of words by taking part in oratorical contests. In his sophomore year he won second place in the Webb Oratorical Contest.

He was also a member of an intercollegiate council formed by some of the white and Negro colleges in Atlanta. The purpose of the council was to encourage friendship among the colleges and to discuss problems of common interest to all college students. It was the first time that Martin had associated with white people as an equal. His experience on the council convinced him that there were many young white people who were on the Negro's side. Until then he had been ready to resent the whole white race.

Martin was a towny. Townies were those students who lived at home. For the first two years he was struggling with a decision. He could not decide what he wanted to do with his life. He had entered Morehouse intending to become a lawyer. He had also thought of studying medicine. But he felt himself being drawn steadily toward the ministry.

His good friend at Morehouse, Walter McCall, who was headed for the seminary after graduation, encouraged Martin to become a minister.

Of course, Reverend King was anxious to have his oldest son enter the ministry. Reverend King had always been a man of strong will. He loved his children dearly and was determined that they should take what he thought were the right roads in life. Even as they approached adulthood, Reverend King continued to try to shield them from the world's evils and to make their decisions for them. His children reacted in different ways to their father's stern advice. Chris, the dutiful daughter, did exactly what her father said. A.D. was rebellious. He was doing badly in college. Eventually he left school and got married. Martin would listen to everything his father had to say and compare it with his own thoughts. He would argue a little, seem to yield a little, and then make up his own mind. Without revealing his decision, he would move toward the goal he had decided upon.

Though the pressures to enter the ministry were great, Martin was repelled by the hand-clapping and shouting characteristic of the Negro church. These reactions were too emotional for his taste. Religion, he believed, should be more intellectual, more thoughtful. He felt that the church should take an interest in man's life on Earth, as well as in the preparation of his soul for Heaven. He believed that the church should concern itself with whether or not a man had his full rights as a human being; whether or not he had a job and enough to eat; whether or not his children were getting a good education.

He could not forget the mission he had set for himself, to attack racial injustice. One thing was certain; whatever road he chose must equip him to achieve this goal.

Dr. Mays was all that Martin wished he could be someday. The Morehouse President was intellectual and yet spiritual. He could deliver an instructive lecture or an uplifting sermon. Dr. Mays usually spoke at the Tuesday chapel sessions. Afterwards Martin would often ask Dr. Mays about the subject covered in chapel.

It was a painful time for Martin. He spent his entire first two years of college asking questions, searching, reading, thinking, discussing.

Finally, when he was a junior in college, he decided to study for the ministry. He told his mother. She sent him to his father. His father received the news with a very solemn face. "We must be sure," he said. He suggested that Martin deliver a trial sermon to a congregation of worshippers.

Seventeen-year-old Martin soon was standing in the pulpit of the Ebenezer Baptist Church. The people crowded into the church to hear his first sermon. His father was very pleased but he said nothing to Martin. That night in his room, where no one could see, Reverend King got down on his knees and thanked God for his son's choice and for his apparent skill.

In 1947 Martin was ordained and named assistant pastor of Ebenezer Baptist Church.

During his summer vacations Martin took jobs that exposed him to the problems of poor black people. With his father's important position in the Negro community, Martin could have gotten an easy office job. Instead he took jobs that required backbreaking work. One summer he worked for Railway Express, unloading trains and trucks. Another summer he worked on a loading gang in a mattress factory. He saw that the problems of the workingman, white or Negro, seemed to be the same. One thing was different. He noticed that Negroes usually were paid less than whites for doing the same job. The smaller paycheck meant that the Negro was lowered to a humbler condition than that of his white fellow worker. The Negro was paid less because he was considered inferior and, Martin realized, Negroes would remain inferior as long as the unequal pay scale continued.

Martin remembered something his sociology teacher, Prof. Walter Chivers, had said again and again in class. "Money is not only the root of evil but also of race." Now Martin saw Prof. Chivers' theory in action.

In the spring of 1948 Martin, a graduating senior, was beginning to develop definite opinions about what education ought to do for the individual. He wrote an article on the subject that was printed in *The Maroon Tiger,* the Morehouse student paper.

The article was entitled "The Purpose of Education." Education should not merely train a person in the technique of doing a certain job. It should not just prepare him to enter a particular occupation either, he wrote. Education should train people to think scientifically and logically. Education should enable a person to be able to tell the true from the false, fact from the fiction. A logical person would lean toward true and worthy goals. A logical person would reject the theory that one race was superior to another.

In June Martin Luther King, Jr., wearing the academic cap and gown, marched in the graduation procession at Morehouse College. He had nearly flunked a French course, but most of his other grades were A's. He won a scholarship to Crozer Theological Seminary in Chester, Pa.

During his college career, he had developed into a sturdy, well-built young man with a serious, thoughtful way about him. He was confident and secure in the knowledge of what his life's work must be. He had become a man. And he now wore a mustache on a face that would soon be one of the most famous in the world.

In the fall he headed north to Crozer. The beautifully landscaped campus is on a small hill. Trees and shrubs set it apart as a place for thought and peace. Crozer had originally been a Baptist school, but its philosophy had since broadened to include most Protestant theologies.

It was Martin's first experience at an integrated school. There were six Negro students in a total student body of 100. He felt watched and judged by the white students. He was determined not to display any of the bad qualities that he knew many white people believed were in all Negroes. Negroes were thought of as always late, always laughing, loud, dirty, and messy. King was grimly serious and quiet. He kept his room immaculate, his shoes shined, his clothes neat. And he tried never to be late for anything.

Among the subjects that he and his classmates studied were church history, the lives and works of the prophets, psychology of religion, and ethics. They learned how to manage a church. They practiced their preaching before each other and in front of the congregations of nearby churches.

Life at Crozer was not all study and deep meditation. The ministers-to-be had their moments of horseplay. One popular joke at Crozer was to sneak into a student's room and turn over every piece of furniture. Everyone, King included, had been a member of such a raiding party at one time or another.

One day the room of a white student from North Carolina was raided. There were other Southern white students at Crozer. But this particular student often used the word "darkie" in conversation. When the North Carolinian discovered his upset room, he went directly to King's room and accused him of doing it. It so happened that King had not been in that raiding party and he said so. The student did not believe him and he pulled out a gun and threatened to shoot King. Other students crowded around him and took the gun. The incident was scheduled to come up before the student government, but King refused to press charges and the matter was dropped. Later the student made a public apology to King.

King was becoming the most admired student on campus. He was thought to be the seminarian-most-likely-to-succeed. He was elected student body president. He was getting all A's and remained at the top of his class during his entire time at Crozer.

As student body president, King had to make many speeches. He was now a speaker whose majesty and dignity captured his audience and overwhelmed it with the ideas he was proposing. The large words he used seemed to have an inner rhythm all their own. Sweeping the students along with this special talent, he became their natural leader.

He no longer was the violent athlete he had been as a boy. One Saturday he was watching a basketball game in the Crozer gym. The players were both Negro and white. The game got rough with elbows jabbing and knees flying. During the third quarter, King stood up and said, "I think it is time for you men to slow the game down." He left the gym. The game calmed.

King entered the social life in nearby Philadelphia, attending parties there and in the suburbs. But he found once again that the North was not the promised land for the Negro. While on a double date, he and his friends were refused service in a Camden (N.J.) restaurant. The owner actually pulled a gun on them. Refusing service to Negroes in public places was against the law in New Jersey. King contacted an NAACP lawyer. But the case was never brought to court because the other patrons in the restaurant refused to be witnesses.

In addition to his classroom work at Crozer, King took some courses in philosophy at the University of Pennsylvania. He read book after book of philosophy. He was searching everywhere for ideas. New ideas were needed to wipe out racial injustice. The old ideas were not working. Fighting injustice with violence seemed only to increase injustice. Fighting injustice only in courts of law was difficult, slow, and sometimes impossible in Southern courts.

King had read 19th-century writer Henry David Thoreau's essay on "Civil Disobedience" at Morehouse. Thoreau argued that no man should cooperate with laws that he feels are unjust. When a man truly feels that a law which society has made is wrong, he should not obey the law. But he must be willing to take the punishment society sets for breaking that law. When society makes unjust laws, the best place for the good man is jail, said Thoreau. This seemed to apply to segregation laws in King's view. Such laws were not only unjust, but they contradicted the U.S. Constitution.

King read Karl Marx, a 19th-century German political philosopher whose teachings started communism. King believed that the dictatorial methods that Marx advocated for wiping out injustice were in themselves wrong. They denied the dignity of man as surely as segregation laws did.

Thoreau's idea of nonviolent resistance seemed a better idea. King continued his search through the writings of the great philosophers. He was looking for a way to use the principles of love and brotherhood as a force against injustice. Once he discovered an acceptable theory, a way to make it work could be found.

One Sunday afternoon King went to Philadelphia to hear a sermon by Dr. Mordecai Johnson. Dr. Johnson was President of Howard University in Washington, D.C. He had been pastor of a church in Charleston, W. Va. He had tried repeatedly to conquer racial injustice by preaching brotherly love, but he found that his words did not move those people who had the power to end injustice.

Dr. Johnson had just returned from India. There he had seen a way to use love as a force for good. On that Sunday in Philadelphia, he told his audience of an Indian named Mohandas K. (Mahatma) Gandhi. Gandhi had freed the Indian people from British rule without approving the firing of a shot or without uttering a violent word. He had used the power of love, Dr. Johnson said. An excited Martin Luther King went back to Crozer that night.

He gathered all the books about Gandhi he could

find. As he read more and more, he knew his search was over. Love could do it. Love could oppose injustice and win.

What did this "love" that Gandhi used mean? It was not the kind of love one has for his mother or sweetheart or child. Perhaps a better word might be respect, respect for a fellow human being because he has the power to think and to hope and to make things better.

In every nonviolent way he could think of, Gandhi had opposed British rule of India. He had refused to pay taxes. He had organized a weaving industry in India so that Indians would not need to depend on Britain for cloth. He led Indians in a dramatic march to the sea to gather salt in defiance of an unjust salt tax. When the British took Gandhi off to jail, he went without protest. Gandhi, too, had read Thoreau.

Gandhi refused to hate the British for their injustice. They were fellow humans. He raised neither hand nor voice against them. He met their persecution with love. And he won.

Gandhi was murdered in 1948, the year of King's graduation from Morehouse. But Gandhi's followers did not allow his ideas to die. And they had transmitted them to Dr. Johnson who then passed them on to King. King would carry them on.

In 1951 King received his Bachelor of Divinity degree from Crozer. He had been an outstanding student. "A very bright young man" and "He seems to know where he wants to go and how to get there," said his professors. He was class valedictorian. He received the school's highest award for scholarship. He was also awarded the Lewis Crozer Fellowship for two years of graduate study in the college of his choice. King chose Boston University.

His parents gave him a new green Chevrolet for a graduation present. When the summer passed, King packed his car with suitcases and boxes and traveled up to Boston University. There he began work on his Doctor of Philosophy degree.

King and Phil Lenud, an old Morehouse classmate who was a student at Tufts University, rented an apartment together. The two students organized the Philo-

"Our far-too-brief moments with him are cherished personal memories, too precious to be adequately described," Mrs. King said after her husband's death.

Dr. King being arrested (above) on a charge of loitering while trying to visit Rev. Ralph Abernathy in a Montgomery, Ala., jail in 1958. Another time racists burned a wooden cross (below) on Dr. King's lawn.

—UPI photo

College students in Greensboro, N.C., take part in a sit-in at a segregated lunch counter in 1960.

—UPI photo

Freedom Riders on buses bound for the South during the early 1960's to protest segregation on buses and in bus stations.

Dr. King, shown here in Albany, Ga., in 1962, often preached nonviolence in poolrooms and taverns.

Birmingham police arrest Dr. King and Reverend Abernathy during a 1963 protest. The marchers wore work clothes as part of an Easter boycott of stores.

—UPI photo

Behind the bars of the Birmingham jail, Dr. King wrote his famous letter in answer to criticism from a group of white clergymen.

—UPI photo

More than 250,000 people gather at the Lincoln Memorial in 1963 to demand equal rights for Negroes.

—Wide World photo

The participants in the 1963 march on Washington hear Dr. King deliver his "I Have a Dream" speech from the steps of the Lincoln Memorial.

Dr. King and other civil rights leaders meet with
President Kennedy after the Washington march.

Dr. King casts his ballot in the 1964 presidential
election after campaigning for President Johnson, the
first political leader whom he actively supported.

—UPI photo

After he refused to leave a segregated restaurant in
St. Augustine, Fla., Dr. King is arrested in 1964.

—Wide World photo

Pope Paul VI meets with Dr. King and Reverend
Abernathy in 1964. The Vatican meeting followed Dr.
King's speeches in East and West Berlin.

—Wide World photos

The Nobel Prize for Peace is awarded to Dr. King (above) at ceremonies in Norway in 1964. Later, his hometown of Atlanta presents Dr. King with an inscribed crystal bowl (below) at a banquet.

A posse attacks students demonstrating for equal voting rights (above) in Montgomery, Ala., in 1965. Freedom marchers (below) trudge through a driving rain on the way from Selma, Ala., to Montgomery.

—UPI photo

Dr. King, James Meredith, Stokely Carmichael, and Floyd McKissick lead a Mississippi march in 1966.

—UPI photo

Singer Joan Baez joins Dr. King in 1966 as he leads children into a newly integrated Mississippi school.

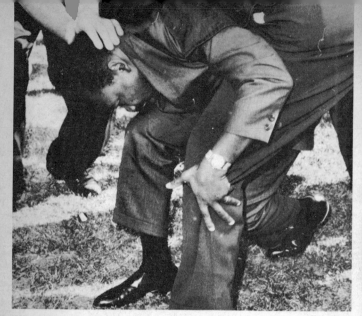

Dr. King after being hit on the head by a rock during a march for open housing in Chicago in 1966.

Dr. Benjamin Spock, the tall white-haired man, and Dr. King lead a parade to protest the Vietnam war.

—UPI photo

School children in Newark, N.J., greet Dr. King in
1968 as he seeks support for the Poor People's
Campaign that he planned to lead in Washington, D.C.

Dr. King standing on the balcony outside his Memphis motel room, talking to staff members the day before he was shot and killed.

Before her husband's funeral Mrs. King and her three oldest children went to Memphis to lead the garbage collectors' march that Dr. King had planned to lead.

—Wide World photo

In Atlanta thousands of mourners follow a mule-drawn casket, symbol of Dr. King's struggle for the poor.

—N.Y. Times photo, Neal Boenzi

Rich and poor Americans, like this New York peddler, shared a common sorrow and loss in Dr. King's death.

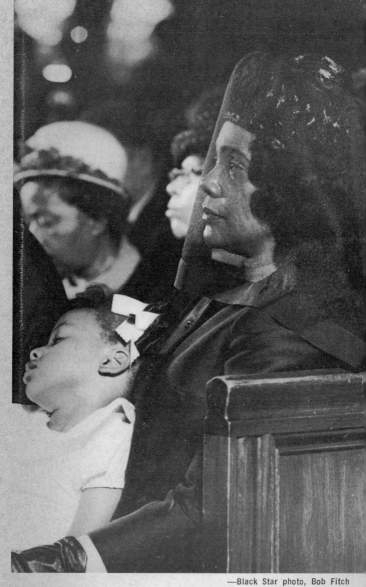

—Black Star photo, Bob Fitch

''We must carry on,'' Mrs. King said, ''because this is the only way he would have wanted it to have been . . . we are going to continue his work. . . .''

sophical Club. Once a week, Negro graduate students from the Boston area would meet to talk and drink coffee. Someone would read an article on a philosophical matter, and the others would discuss it and try to prove or disprove the article. The club became so well-known in college circles that soon white students were attending the sessions too.

King had been in Boston only a few months when he met Coretta Scott. She was a graduate student at the New England Conservatory of Music. Miss Scott had been born in Heiberger, Ala., not far from Selma. She had done her undergraduate work at Ohio's Antioch College. Now the attractive soprano was preparing herself for a career as a concert singer.

King made up his mind about her on their first date. They had gone to lunch together. "You have some great hair," he said as he surveyed her long dark hair. As they talked, the conversation turned to sociology, and Miss Scott had definite thoughts on the subject. After she had expressed her views, her date was impressed. "You can talk about other things than music . . . about ideas," said King.

As he drove her home in his green Chevrolet that day, King astonished Miss Scott by saying, "You have all of the qualities that I expect to find in the girl I'd like to have for a wife."

Miss Scott was also impressed with King. She thought him a gentleman and not at all the bore she believed most intellectuals were. But she was not sure she wanted to marry a minister. Being a minister's wife did not fit in with the future she had planned for herself as a glamorous soprano rushing from concert to concert, accepting flowers onstage, going out for midnight suppers with handsome men.

In the months that followed, King and Miss Scott dated regularly. They went to concerts and movies together. They would drive over to Boston's Western Lunch Box for a meal of King's favorite dish, greens and ham hocks. Often they would study together. The more Miss Scott saw of him, the more she liked him. Soon she began to realize that she would not be happy without him. They were married on June 18, 1953, in her parents' garden in Heiberger, Ala. The couple returned to Boston after the wedding to complete their studies.

King finished his course at Boston University, and began to research the thesis that was part of the requirement for his doctoral degree. The thesis would attempt to settle a controversy that had been continuing among philosophers for almost 20 years. Dr. Paul Tillich, a German professor, and Dr. Henry Wieman, an American, disagreed over the nature of God. It was King's job to summarize the writings of these two men and to attempt to clarify the controversy.

Mrs. King graduated from the conservatory in June 1954. By the end of the summer King had finished all work toward earning his degree, except for his thesis. During that year he had been considering various positions offered by universities and churches. He had been offered a deanship, an administrative position, and a teaching post by different colleges. He had offers from two Northern churches and invitations from two Southern churches.

King's ideal was to be a teacher-minister like Dr. Benjamin Mays. He felt, though, that he needed the experience of ministering to a church before he could teach. The Kings considered the question of whether to settle in the North or the South. Though not perfect, the North was a much freer place for Negroes to live. But the Kings had fond memories of the South, despite its problems. The experience and education they both had might help to solve those problems. They decided that it was their duty to go back to the South.

King accepted the invitation of Dexter Avenue Baptist Church in Montgomery, Ala., to give a trial sermon shortly after Christmas. The Dexter congregation consisted mainly of teachers from Alabama State College. As he prepared his sermon, he could not decide whether he should try to impress them with scholarship or simply depend on the inspiration of God as he usually did. Finally he said to himself, "Keep Martin Luther King in the background and God in the foreground and everything will be all right." Dexter Avenue Church must have liked the sermon. A month later they invited him to be the pastor of their church.

Montgomery had been the capital of the Confederacy during the Civil War. Life for Negroes in Montgomery was considered by many as being the worst in the South. Segregation was rigid, good-paying jobs were few. Negro voter registration was discouraged by slow and tedious processing procedures. Negroes were not permitted to sit in the first four rows of seats on buses. This meant that when the bus was crowded, Negroes had to stand over empty seats. For years, educated and uneducated Negroes had raised scarcely a word of protest against the injustices they lived with every day.

On May 17, 1954, the Supreme Court ordered all schools desegregated. As the summer of 1954 wore on, voices were being raised and stirrings were being heard in the Negro community of Montgomery.

In September 1954, the Kings moved into the parsonage on South Jackson Street. Mrs. King busied herself with arranging and organizing the parsonage into a home and with getting to know the ladies of the church. King familiarized himself with church routine. He reorganized the church budget. He organized a parish Social and Political Action Committee to encourage the congregation to take a more active role in community affairs. One of the committee's first jobs was to set up a voting clinic. In the voting clinic unregistered voters of the congregation were trained to avoid the traps of red tape that registrars set for Negro voters.

Meanwhile, King continued to work on his thesis. By the spring of 1955, he had completed it. His research had led him to the conclusion that Tillich believed God was power and being while Wieman believed God was goodness and value. His thesis was approved, and on June 5, 1955, he was awarded a Ph.D. degree by Boston University.

A few days before he became Doctor King, on May 31, the Supreme Court reaffirmed its 1954 decision and ordered all schools in the land desegregated "with all deliberate speed." This action angered many Southern whites. They organized White Citizens' Councils to counteract the court order.

On August 28 Emmett Till, a 14-year-old Chicago boy who was visiting relatives in Mississippi, was kidnapped and lynched. Negroes and whites were horrified. Unrest, anger, and impatience grew in the Negro community in the following months. And then December 1, 1955, dawned in Montgomery, Ala.

Chapter VII

Montgomery:
Sore Feet
On A Crowded Bus

Early evening on Thursday, December 1, 1955, was unseasonably warm in Montgomery, Ala. The stores were closing and early Christmas shoppers poured out into the streets. As the Cleveland Avenue bus pulled to a stop near the Montgomery Fair, a large department store, Mrs. Rosa Parks got on. The dignified, 43-year-old Negro woman worked as a seamstress in the Montgomery Fair. She had done some shopping after work and her feet hurt.

The bus was filling up. Mrs. Parks was lucky enough to find a seat near the front, one row behind the section reserved for white passengers. She sat down and eased the heel of her shoe off for just a second. Ahhh, that was better.

The bus proceeded along its route, passing through Court Square. By the time the bus pulled up to the stop in front of the Empire Theater, there were no seats left on the bus. Six white passengers boarded the bus. As was the normal practice, the driver turned to the Negroes sitting just behind the white section and said, "Let me have those seats." Three Negro passengers got up at once. But Mrs. Parks did not move. Suddenly she forgot her skin color. She became a human being whose feet hurt and who had found a seat on a crowded bus. She did not budge. The driver asked her again, but still she refused to move.

The driver got off the bus and called the police. When the officers arrived, Mrs. Parks looked up at one of them and said quietly, "Why do you push us around?" "I don't know," said the officer, "but the law is the law and you're under arrest."

For the crime of not giving up her seat to a white man, Mrs. Parks, a respected member of the Negro community, was taken to jail. There, she was fingerprinted and booked. She was charged with violating the city's segregation law. During the past year alone, five Negro women and two Negro children had been arrested for disobeying bus drivers. One man had been shot to death by a policeman for the same offense.

Mrs. Parks had been a secretary of the local branch of the NAACP. When Mr. E. D. Nixon, head of the state NAACP, heard of her arrest, he immediately went down to the jail and posted bail for her release. Nixon was a pullman porter who despite his lack of education managed to make a good living for his family. He was one of the few Negroes in Montgomery who had been raising his voice against segregation for years.

News of Mrs. Parks's arrest spread quickly throughout the Negro community. After many phone calls several influential Negro women got the idea of a bus boycott. The idea was passed on to Nixon who thought that it was a good one.

Before retiring that night, Nixon sat on the edge of his bed for a long time, thinking. After a while he turned to his wife and said, "You know, I think every Negro in town should stay off the buses for one day in protest for Mrs. Parks's arrest." His wife looked at him as if she thought he was crazy. Then Nixon said, "What do you think?" His wife said, "I think you ought to stop day dreaming and turn out that light and get some sleep."

Early Friday morning Nixon called Dr. Martin Luther King, Jr. Excitedly, without bothering to say hello, Nixon poured out the story of Mrs. Parks's arrest and jailing. His voice trembling, Nixon concluded by saying, "We have taken this type of thing too long already. I feel that the time has come to boycott the buses. Only through a boycott can we make it clear to the white folks that we will not accept this type of treatment any longer." Dr. King agreed with the idea of a boycott.

Following his conversation with Nixon, Dr. King called Rev. Ralph Abernathy, who was the pastor of Montgomery's First Baptist Church. Reverend Abernathy was to become one of the leaders in the events that followed and a close friend of Dr. King's. The two men would work well together in the coming months and years. Reverend Abernathy was the man of action and organization; Dr. King, the man who could inspire and lead people. The two ministers agreed that a boycott should be organized. They contacted other ministers and civic leaders and arranged a meeting for that evening. Dr. King suggested that the meeting be held at his church.

Saturday night was another warm night as 40 Negroes from every walk of life gathered at Dexter Avenue Baptist Church. Rev. L. Roy Bennett was appointed chairman. He opened the meeting by saying that all Negroes should boycott the buses on Monday, Dec. 5. Then he said, "Now is the time to move. This is no time to talk; it is the time to act." For a while the determined minister would not let anyone talk, make a suggestion, or ask a question. But the others protested and threatened to leave if they were not allowed to speak.

Then the questions came. How long should the boycott last? How would the Negro community be informed of the boycott? How would people get to work if they did not ride the buses? But everyone agreed that there should be a boycott.

It was decided to hold a mass meeting on Monday evening. There, a vote would be taken to decide how long the boycott would last.

A few leaflets proposing a boycott had already been distributed that afternoon. It was agreed to print more and distribute them the next afternoon. Dr. King offered to have the leaflets mimeographed in his church. The leaflets said: "Don't ride the bus to work, to town, to school, or anyplace Monday, December 5. Another Negro woman has been arrested and put in jail because she refused to give up her bus seat. Come to a mass meeting Monday at 7 p.m. at the Holt Street Baptist Church for further instructions."

The 18 Negro taxi companies in the city with 210 taxis in all were asked to carry people for the same dime fare that the people paid on the bus.

The ministers present agreed to urge their congregations on Sunday morning to participate in the boycott. The next morning Dr. King was up early and by 9 o'clock he and the church secretary had turned out 7,000 leaflets. At 11 a.m. a large group of women and children set off to distribute them.

The Negroes were given some unexpected help in spreading the word of the boycott by a white newspaper, *The Montgomery Advertiser*. The newspaper learned of the boycott when a white subscriber sent them one of the leaflets distributed on Friday afternoon. The newspaper printed the story on the front page of the Saturday morning edition. The intention was to let the white people know what the Negroes were up to, but the story also served to inform the entire Negro community of the boycott.

The following day Dr. King went about his usual Sunday church duties at Dexter Avenue Church. Late that evening he sat down to read the paper. He noticed a long article in the paper about the proposed boycott. The article compared the boycott to the methods of the White Citizens' Council whose avowed purpose was to preserve segregation. Those methods were terror, threats, and often economic reprisals. A boycott is one method of economic reprisal since it threatens the income of a business.

Dr. King was troubled by the article. Was a boycott unchristian? Was it an ethical technique? Even if it brought about justice, was it right? He realized that it was the goal that was important, and the means to that goal were nonviolent. No one would be physically injured; no property would be destroyed. The Negroes' concern was not to put the bus company out of business but to put justice into the business. Segregation was an evil, and to go along with it was to help it to continue, he concluded.

He thought of Thoreau's essay on "Civil Disobedience" that he had read in college. He said softly to himself, "We are simply saying to the white community, 'We can no longer cooperate with an evil system. We will use noncooperation to give birth to justice.'"

Dr. King went to bed early that night but he was scarcely asleep when his two-week-old daughter Yoki started to cry. Then the phone started to ring and ring.

Around midnight a committee member called to say that all of the taxi companies had agreed to cooperate in transporting people to work. Finally there was silence in the King household and sleep came.

By 5:30 Monday morning, Dec. 5, the Kings were up and dressed. Of the 17,500 Negro bus riders in the city, how many would not ride the bus that day? How many Negroes would stick together in a city that had been plagued by Negro defeatism for years? Dr. King's estimate was that 60 percent would be a good showing.

There was a bus stop just a few feet from the King home and the Kings began an impatient watch at the window. The first bus was scheduled to pass the house at 6 o'clock. Dr. King decided to go into the kitchen for a cup of coffee.

Suddenly he heard Mrs. King call out from the living room, "Martin, Martin, come quickly." As he ran into the living room, Mrs. King pointed to the window and said, "It's empty, darling, it's empty." They could hardly believe it. The South Jackson line, which ran past their house, was usually packed with Negro domestic workers at that hour.

In 15 minutes another bus was scheduled to pass the house. They waited. It, too, was empty. A third bus passed. The only passengers were two white people.

Dr. King jumped into his car and cruised down every main street, searching the windows of the buses. In all, he saw eight Negro passengers. It was true. It was really true. The Negro community of Montgomery had united at last to fight for their rights and dignity.

Negroes thumbed rides. They shared their cars. They rode mules. They walked. Some, past middle age, walked as much as 12 miles that day. But they did not ride the buses.

Motorcycle patrolmen trailed the buses, for some white people were certain that Negro goon squads had been organized to force other Negroes to stay off the buses. The only person they were able to hang the goon charge on was a college student who was helping an old lady across the street.

Monday was also the day of Mrs. Parks's trial. She was found guilty of disobeying the segregation law and was fined $14. Her conviction only served to stiffen the resolve of the boycotters.

At 3 o'clock that afternoon a small meeting was called by Reverend Bennett to make plans for the mass meeting that evening. At the meeting it was decided to create a formal organization to conduct the boycott. Reverend Abernathy suggested the name Montgomery Improvement Association (MIA). A president was elected to lead the organization, Dr. Martin Luther King, Jr. A nonviolent protest, which was not even his idea, had singled him out as its leader. For years he had prepared himself. He had thought. He had listened. He had studied. He was ready.

The new organization turned to plans for the mass meeting that night. At first it was thought wise to keep all plans for the boycott concealed from the newspaper reporters who would almost certainly attend the meeting. It was suggested that if there were any decisions concerning strategy they would be mimeographed and passed out secretly during the meeting. A long discussion followed. Finally, E. D. Nixon said, "We are acting like little boys. If we are afraid, we might as well fold up right now. We must be men enough to discuss our plans in the open; this idea of secretly passing papers around is a lot of bunk. The white folks are going to find it out anyway. We'd better decide now if we are going to be fearless men or scared boys." The fear that had threatened the new organization disappeared.

Although the mass meeting at Holt Street Church that night was not scheduled to begin until 7 o'clock, people began to come long before that. By 5 o'clock the church was packed with people. By 7 o'clock there was a traffic jam that extended for five blocks in every direction. As the meeting began, about 4,000 people were gathered outside the church.

The meeting opened with the singing of "Onward, Christian Soldiers." Inside and outside, they sang in a mighty chorus. It was as though all creation were being officially informed of the events to come and of the spirit that would make the world change.

Dr. King addressed the crowd. "We are tired," he told the crowd, "tired of being segregated and humiliated. We are impatient for justice. But we will protest with love. There will be no violence on our part. There will be no cross burnings. No white person will be taken from his home by a hooded Negro mob and murdered. If we do this, if we protest with love, future historians will have to say, 'There lived a great people, a black people, who injected new meaning and dignity into the veins of civilization.' "

The crowd applauded long after he had taken his seat.

Reverend Abernathy then read the resolution to be presented to the bus and city officials. No Negro would ride the buses until courteous treatment of Negroes by drivers was guaranteed; until passenger seating was changed to a first-come, first-served basis, Negroes from the back of the bus, white people from the front of the bus; until Negro bus drivers were employed to drive the predominantly Negro routes. "All in favor, stand up," Reverend Abernathy said. Every single person stood up, and those standing raised their hands. Montgomery, Ala. got ready to take its place in American history along with Lexington and Concord.

Present that night was a young white minister, Rev. Robert Graetz, the pastor of a Negro Lutheran church. He was the only white member of the MIA. In the months to follow the sandy-haired, energetic minister was to stand beside his Negro brothers in their darkest and brightest hours.

The day after the mass meeting the MIA took up the organization of committees to handle the problems and needs of the Negro boycotters.

It was obvious that the arrangement with the Negro taxis could only be temporary for they would soon begin to feel the profit loss. The MIA had also discovered that there was a city ordinance that set a minimum taxi fare. A transportation committee was set up immediately to organize a car pool.

Drivers were recruited at weekly mass meetings. The response was tremendous. Over 150 drivers volunteered at one meeting. Using a map of the city, the committee plotted the location of pick-up stations where people could meet when they needed a ride.

The city invoked the minimum fare ordinance for taxis on December 9. By Tuesday, Dec. 13, the MIA had worked out a car-pool system that functioned, as the white opposition was to admit later, "with military precision."

Housewives, laborers, college professors, dignified gray-haired ladies driving Cadillacs, white and Negro airmen from a nearby air base transported the former bus riders to and from their jobs. Many white housewives picked up their Negro maids every morning and took them home at night. They were not about to be deprived of the services of their maids, boycott or no boycott.

Some people preferred to walk, feeling that it was a symbolic act in the struggle for justice. One driver stopped alongside an elderly black lady who was slowly making her way down the street. "Let me give you a ride; you don't need to walk," he said to her. But she waved him on. "I'm not walking for myself," she explained. "I'm walking for my children and grandchildren."

Gas for the car pool, as well as other expenses, cost the MIA $5,000 a month. At first the boycott was supported by the Negroes of Montgomery, rich and poor. As newspapers spread the word of the stand being taken in Montgomery, the checks began to pour in from all over the country and the world. Churches in nearly every city in the United States sent contributions. Support came from labor unions. Money came from as far away as Tokyo; from Singapore, from Switzerland, from ships at sea. With the checks came notes of encouragement. "Your work is outstanding in the history of our country." "You have shown that decency and courage will eventually prevail." "The entire nation salutes you."

Eventually, ten office workers were needed to handle the tremendous amounts of mail. Soon it was possible to buy a fleet of 15 station wagons to be used in the car pool. After a series of moves the MIA finally found adequate office space in the Bricklayers Union Building.

One of the hardest jobs was holding the people together. This task fell mainly to Dr. King. He gave the people a philosophy. He convinced them that they were in the right and that they would succeed. He told the people that to meet hate with hate would do nothing but intensify the existence of evil. From hate comes more hate; from violence comes more violence. "We must meet the forces of hate with the power of love," he said. "Above all, our aim must never be to defeat or humiliate the white man, but to win his friendship and understanding."

At first this philosophy was hard for many to accept. Nonviolence to them meant cowardice. They would say, "If nobody hits me, I will hit nobody. But if I am hit, I will hit back." Although some never really understood nonviolence, they soon learned that nonviolence was not for cowards.

The city and bus officials were sure that the first rainy day would find the Negroes back on the buses. But the rainy day came and went and still the boycotters held firm. At this point, the officials notified MIA that they were ready to discuss Negro grievances.

The meeting was held on December 8. MIA presented its resolutions, which had been voted on at the first mass meeting. The bus company agreed to guarantee courtesy to Negro passengers. This had been promised many times before, but bus drivers had continued to abuse Negroes with words and actions. Even though the other MIA demands did not ask for the abolishment of segregation, they were politely turned down.

As the boycott continued, meeting followed meeting, but neither side gave an inch. Dr. King learned something very important from these fruitless meetings. He began to see that he had expected the city and bus officials to discuss the issues just as his college professors had so freely done. Clear thinking would settle their differences, he was sure. Now he could see that an agreement hinged not on thought but on power. The privileged were not about to give away their privileges just because the unprivileged asked for them.

There was power in the boycott and so it continued. The white officials began to see that the Negroes were united and determined to hold firm. The officials turned to other means of dealing with their opponents. They started rumors that the leaders of the MIA were misusing MIA money. They gave a false story to the newspapers that a settlement had been reached. Through the Associated Press, MIA learned of the story before it appeared in the Montgomery paper. MIA representatives went into bars and churches and warned the Negroes that the story was false and that the boycott was not over.

In a "get tough" policy, the Mayor went on television and denounced the boycott. The city commissioners publicly joined the segregationist White Citizens' Council.

Many car-pool drivers were threatened with the loss of their licenses and cancellation of their insurance. Negroes waiting for rides were threatened with vagrancy charges if they did not move on. One afternoon after Dr. King had picked up three riders on his way home, he was trailed by two motorcycle policemen. The officers stopped him, searched him, and took him to jail on a charge of going 30 mph in a 25 mph zone. When Negroes heard of Dr. King's arrest, they gathered threateningly outside the jail. The jailer released Dr. King on his own bond.

From the time the boycott began, the Kings received threats by phone and by letter. After the Mayor's "get tough" television appearance, the threats increased. Dr. King did not take the threats seriously until several white friends told him that they had gotten wind of a plot to kill him.

One night, just after Dr. King had gone to bed, the phone rang. A voice at the other end said, "Listen nigger, we've taken all we want from you; before next week you'll be sorry you ever came to Montgomery." Dr. King hung up on the caller. He found himself drained of all courage. He went into the kitchen for a cup of coffee. And he prayed aloud. "I am taking a stand for what I believe is right. But now I am afraid. The people are looking to me for leadership, but I have no more courage."

Then an inner voice, which seemed to him to be the presence of God, said, "Stand up for the right; I am with you."

Almost at once, he was no longer afraid. He was ready to face anything.

Three evenings later, while Mrs. King and the wife of a church member were watching television in the living room, there was a thud on the front porch. Dr. King was away for the evening, talking to a mass meeting. The noise sounded like a brick to Mrs. King. But some instinct told her to move to the back part of the house.

As they moved toward the back room where nine-week-old Yoki was sleeping, the "brick" went off. It was a bomb. The force of the explosion split one of the pillars on the porch, broke the front windows, and filled the living room with broken glass. The house filled with smoke. Mrs. King rushed into the baby's room. Then the doorbell rang. "Now they are coming in," she thought to herself. She could not think what to do to protect the baby. Then she heard the front door open and a neighbor's voice say, "Is anybody hurt?" The phone began to ring and the neighbor answered it. A woman's voice said, "Yes, I did it. I'm just sorry I didn't kill all of you."

Dr. King was informed at once of the bombing. By the time he arrived at the shattered parsonage, an angry crowd of Negroes had gathered outside. They were holding guns, rocks, rods, knives, sticks, and bottles. Nonviolence was plainly not what they had on their minds. Dr. King went inside to be sure that his family was all right. He returned quickly to speak to the people outside. It was clear that Montgomery teetered on the edge of a blood bath that night.

Standing in front of his wrecked home, Dr. King told his fellow Negroes just how deeply he believed in nonviolence. "Get rid of your weapons," he said. "We must love our white brothers, no matter what they do to us. What we are doing is just, and God is with us." The curses and shouts that had filled the air before he began to speak were replaced by "Amens." An old man in the crowd called out, "God bless you, Son." In twos and threes, the now peaceful crowd began to break up.

Shortly after the bombing of King's home, the MIA realized that there could be no justice within the unjust system of segregation. On February 1, they filed a suit in the U.S. Federal District Court asking that segregation on buses be abolished because it violated the 14th Amendment to the U.S. Constitution. The hearing was set for May 11.

In the meantime, the city indicted 115 Negroes, Dr. King among them. The charge was conspiracy to destroy a business. Many of the civic, religious, and educational leaders of the Negro community were named on the list of the indictments. There were 24 ministers named. At first the Negro community was shocked. But then they began to see how ridiculous it was that many of the most respected Negroes in Montgomery had suddenly been accused of a crime.

The case came to trial on March 19, and on March 22 Dr. King, the first of the defendants to be tried, was found guilty of the charge and fined $500. The trial and conviction became the center of the country's attention. Reporters swarmed into Montgomery. The news that respectable people peacefully pressing for justice should be branded as criminals caused many Americans to react. The arrests also served to draw the besieged boycotters even closer together.

Dr. Martin Luther King, Jr. had begun to emerge as a national leader. *The Hartford* (Conn.) *Courant* was one of the first to recognize this. On March 10, 1956, an editorial said in part, "Emerging from the racial conflict in Montgomery, Alabama, is the growing leadership of a Negro clergyman, Martin Luther King. By virtue of his intelligence and piety Mr. King has gradually become the spokesman for passive resistance. It is well to remember his name. For if this movement is successful, as it appears likely, the Reverend Dr. King will become not only a national hero among his race, but the continuing spearhead in the fight against segregation."

On June 4 the U.S. Federal District Court, acting on the suit filed by MIA members, found that the city bus segregation laws of Alabama were unconstitutional. Attorneys for the city took the case to the Supreme Court in Washington.

Throughout the summer the car pools rolled and the buses remained empty as all Montgomery and the nation awaited the news from Washington.

In the meantime, the city decided to launch a legal attack on the car pool. The car pool was declared a "public nuisance." Dr. King and other leaders of the boycott were charged with operating a private enterprise without a license. The hearing was set for November 13.

November 13 came and still there was no news from Washington. The spirits of the boycotters were low. If the trial declared the car pool illegal, they were beaten. The first morning of testimony proceeded. Just at noon, Dr. King and the MIA attorneys noticed a commotion in the back of the courtroom. A reporter came rushing up to Dr. King with a piece of paper. "Here is the decision you have been waiting for. Read this release."

Dr. King read the words, "The United States Supreme Court today affirmed a decision of a special three-judge U.S. District Court in declaring Alabama's state and local laws requiring segregation on buses unconstitutional."

They had won. The car-pool drivers, the elderly ladies who preferred to walk, the telephone committees, the leaflet printers, all of them had waged a battle and had won. Negroes of Montgomery could now enjoy the view from the front of the bus.

Although the trial proceeded and found the car pool illegal, a share-the-ride plan was worked out by the boycotters until the court order could be delivered to the city officials.

On December 21, 1956, Dr. King got on the South Jackson Street bus. He took a seat next to the window. Rev. Glenn Smiley, a white minister from New York, got on and sat down next to Dr. King. White man and black man, side by side in Montgomery, Alabama, went for a ride on the bus.

Chapter VIII

SCLC:
The New Leader

Dr. King was the black man of the hour in January 1957. Although integration of the buses in Montgomery had been followed by a brief reign of terror, the triumph was complete. Newspapers, radio, and television had told the world of the victory and of the victorious general, Dr. King.

He was showered with honors and awards. At 28, he became the youngest person ever to win the Spingarn Medal, which is awarded annually to the person making the greatest contribution in race relations. He spoke before the platform committee of the Democratic National Convention. *Time* magazine ran a cover story on him. Colleges and churches sought him as their head.

Along with other prominent Negro and white Americans, Dr. and Mrs. King were invited to the independence ceremonies of Ghana, the first black African nation to be freed by a colonial power (Great Britain). Their visit to Africa was a highly emotional one for the Kings. They found it awesome to walk the earth where their ancestors walked.

In June 1957 Morehouse College became the first of many colleges to award Dr. King an honorary degree. Only nine years before, he had received his Bachelor of Arts degree from Morehouse President, Dr. Benjamin Mays. As Dr. King stood again on the same platform, Dr. Mays read from the citation that accompanied the degree. "You led the people with quiet dignity, Christian grace, and determined purpose. While you were away, your colleagues in the battle for freedom were being arrested like criminals. [Montgomery, February 1956] When it was suggested that you might stay away and avoid arrest, I heard you say, 'I would rather spend ten years in jail than desert the people in this crisis.' At that moment, my heart, my mind, and my soul stood up erect and saluted you." Thus Dr. Mays, who had been young Martin Luther King's ideal, saluted his former student.

Aside from the honors, another result of the success in Montgomery was that many Negroes now looked to Dr. King for leadership. Southern Negro leaders wanted to know how to conduct a bus boycott in "the Montgomery way." It seemed a tood time to unite the efforts of Southern Negroes.

A conference was called to meet at Ebenezer Baptist Church on January 10-11, 1957. Representatives from ten Southern states attended. Out of this conference came a new organization called the Southern Christian Leadership Conference (SCLC). SCLC asked all Negroes "to assert their human dignity by refusing further cooperation with evil." Dr. King was elected SCLC President.

A series of successful bus boycotts in Tallahassee, Atlanta, and other Southern cities followed. When the buses in Atlanta were desegregated, one of the ministers was quoted as saying, "Thank you, Montgomery. Thank you, Dr. Martin Luther King."

The Gandhian technique of nonviolence was proving to be a powerful weapon in the Negro struggle for equality. But Dr. King's goal and Gandhi's goals were different. Gandhi had opposed the rule of his country by a foreign country and thus opposed all British laws as unjust. But Dr. King was a loyal American who believed that Negroes as Americans were guaranteed their rights by the U.S. Constitution. Local segregation laws were unjust because they interfered with a Negro American's constitutional rights. Dr. King opposed only segregation laws.

Dr. King looked to Washington for support and enforcement of constitutional rights for his people. Together with Roy Wilkins, NAACP Executive Secretary, and A. Phillip Randolph, head of the railroad porters union and long a civil rights pioneer, Dr. King called for a Prayer Pilgrimage to Washington. And the people came. By train, bus, and automobile, more than 35,000 persons, 10 percent of them white, came to stand before the Lincoln Memorial and listen to speeches. It was May 17, 1957, the third anniversary of the Supreme Court decision that had declared segregated schools unconstitutional.

There were speeches by Dr. Mordecai Johnson, Phillip Randolph, and Congressman Adam Clayton Powell. Then Randolph said, "I give you Martin Luther King." As Dr. King, wearing a black robe, approached the microphone, the people rose as one, waving handkerchiefs and programs. With the likeness of Abraham Lincoln, the Great Emancipator, behind him, Dr. King called upon President Dwight Eisenhower to take a stand for the constitutional rights of Negroes. He called upon the Congress to pass laws which would protect Negroes' rights. How could this be done? By enforcing Negro voting rights. "Give us the ballot," he cried again and again, each time following the demand with a story of an injustice caused by violation of Negro voting rights. When Dr. King finished, the people stood and sang "America" and the largest civil rights demonstration that America had yet seen was over.

As a follow-up to the Prayer Pilgrimage, SCLC and the NAACP organized a Crusade for Citizenship. Its goal was to register five million new Negro voters in the South.

But there was silence from the White House. White segregationist resistance to integration grew. Southern states were passing new segregation laws. Through speeches and articles, Dr. King pleaded for presidential support. Finally, after talking with Vice-President Richard Nixon, a meeting was arranged with President Eisenhower for the following year.

In the meantime, the school integration crisis in Little Rock, Ark., erupted. The President found it necessary to send federal troops to Little Rock to protect the Negro students who were attending a white school for the first time.

The White House conference was held on June 23, 1958. Dr. King and three other civil rights leaders attended. They presented a nine-point proposal to the President. The proposal asked that the President take the lead in directing government agencies and departments to protect the civil rights of Negroes. They asked that he take a strong stand against federal financial support of segregated schools and hospitals. They asked that the President direct the Justice Department to assure the prosecution of those who bomb and murder Negroes.

President Eisenhower made little official response to these requests. He said he thought that the answer was to change men's hearts. He did not say how this might be done or what Negroes were supposed to do until hearts changed. The President did not agree to any part of the proposal nor did he offer any compromise that day. To Dr. King, the President was a good, sincere man who had no idea of the problems that Negroes lived with from day to day.

Dr. King turned back to his own resources. He suggested stand-ins at the Southern polling places. He continued to direct the work of the Crusade for Citizenship.

In September of 1958, Dr. King's work was interrupted and almost ended. He had written a book called *Stride for Freedom*, which was the story of the Montgomery struggle. He was sitting at a desk in a Harlem department store autographing copies of the book. A heavyset Negro woman approached him. Cursing, she plunged a letter opener deep into the right side of his chest. The point of the steel blade penetrated to the outer wall of the aorta, the body's main artery. Dr. King was taken to the hospital with the letter opener still in his chest. After three hours of delicate surgery, during which it was necessary to cut away part of one rib, the letter opener was removed.

The woman was captured as she tried to run from the store. Hysterically, she babbled that Dr. King was a Communist and that he had tried to convert her from Catholicism. She was taken to jail and later committed to a hospital for the criminally insane.

Later, Dr. King condemned the climate of hate and bitterness that approved and thus brought on such violent acts. He forgave the woman.

By early 1959 Dr. King was fully recovered. He decided to visit India, the land Gandhi helped free. India's

Prime Minister Jawaharlal Nehru had repeatedly invited the Kings to visit India, but Dr. King had never had the time.

Dr. and Mrs. King and their friend Lawrence Reddick arrived in New Delhi on February 10, 1959. In a speech shortly after his arrival, Dr. King said, "To other countries I may go as a tourist, but to India, I come as a pilgrim."

Dr. King visited Gandhi's shrine in New Delhi. In 1929, the year of Dr. King's birth, Gandhi had sent a message to American Negroes. "Let not the 12 million Negroes be ashamed of the fact that they are the grand-children of slaves. There is no dishonor in being slaves. There is dishonor in being slave owners. But let us not think of past honor or dishonor . . . the future is with those who would be truthful, pure, and loving. . . ." Now in February 1959, Dr. King, an unashamed descendant of slaves who believed in the power of love, stood at the grave of Gandhi.

Dr. King was impressed by the Prime Minister's con-demnation of the oppression of the untouchables in India. For centuries the untouchables, at the bottom of India's caste system, had been segregated and dis-criminated against. Now, Nehru was urging his country-men to stop this ancient cruelty. Dr. King could not help but compare the words and actions of this man to America's own President who seemed to be deaf to Negro cries for support of their rights.

When he returned to the U.S., Dr. King found a country in distress.

In the South segregationists had unleashed a cam-paign of bombings, beatings, and finally a lynching. They openly defied the Civil Rights Commission and other federal agencies.

Negroes had been filled with hope after Montgomery. Now, with mounting anger, they were declaring their impatience for equality. Some were listening to the words of hate and black separatism which Elijah Mu-hammed issued from his Black Muslim headquarters in Chicago. Negro youths were staging mass marches on Washington.

What were they feeling, these Negroes? A young civil

rights leader said, "This is . . . the age of sputniks as well as the age of urban sprawl. Negroes have emerged from two . . . world wars with a new dimension of personal significance. They are no longer willing to be half-slave and half-free."

It seemed certain that one day very soon, the violent segregationists and the impatient Negroes would collide. Somebody had to do something.

Dr. King decided that he could no longer devote himself part-time to SCLC. In a sermon to the Dexter Avenue congregation, he resigned as pastor. Gripping the sides of the pulpit, he said, "I can't stop now. History has thrust something upon me from which I cannot turn away. I should free you now."

In January 1960, Dr. King moved his family to Atlanta. There he assumed the assistant pastorship of Ebenezer Baptist Church, his father's church. Now he gave more time to SCLC.

One impatient Negro asserted his dignity on February 1, 1960, in Greensboro, N.C. On that day Joseph McNeil, a Negro college student, was refused service at a lunch counter in a Woolworth store. He complained about this to his roommate. "There's nothing you can do about it," said the roommate.

But Joseph McNeil disagreed. He and three of his friends returned to the lunch counter, determined to sit there until they were either served or arrested. Each day they returned to sit. The sit-in technique was not new. It had been started and used successfully off and on by a civil rights group called the Congress of Racial Equality (CORE). But McNeil's sit-in touched off a gigantic sit-in movement among college students.

Eight days later, students in Charlotte staged a sit-in. The movement spread to other cities in North Carolina, then across the South. Day after day, the students sat at lunch counters, silently waiting to be served. They sat motionless while heckling whites poured catsup on their clothes and salt in their hair. Many were arrested on the charge of trespassing. When arrested, they refused to pay fines, preferring in the tradition of Thoreau to go to jail.

In Tallahassee, Fla., when a weeping mother begged

to pay her daughter's fine, the daughter firmly insisted that she preferred to stay in jail. She said, "Mamma, I love you. But I'm not free. And I'm not free because your generation didn't act. But I want my children to be free. That's why I'll stay in jail."

When the students got out of jail, they returned to sit again. Sit-ins spread to department stores, supermarkets, theaters, and libraries. By 1961 3,600 students had been arrested for sitting-in. As a result of their efforts, one or more lunch counters in 108 Southern communities had desegregated by 1961.

Dr. King had been a hero to many of the students during their teen-age years. Now they turned to him and SCLC for leadership and guidance. Dr. King and other SCLC officials felt that the students should have an organization of their own.

A conference of student sit-in leaders was called for April 15-17 at Shaw University in Raleigh, N.C. In his opening address to the students, Dr. King emphasized that the students should look deeper into the philosophy of nonviolence. Nonviolence must seek harmony, cooperation, and justice in a community. The use of nonviolence without the spirit of nonviolence could well become a new kind of violence, he said.

Out of the conference came the Student Nonviolent Coordinating Committee (SNCC). But the students did not follow Dr. King's advice. They used nonviolence as a technique, but they did not seek the friendship of the segregationist. Power was what they wanted. The membership of CORE reflected the same feeling. CORE, organized in 1943, was undergoing rapid growth in the early 1960's.

During this time the losers in Alabama took another legal poke at Dr. King. They accused him of falsifying his income tax. Dr. King's defense attorney was able to prove that the state's case rested on a mathematical trick. The prosecution had no answer to this contention. After nearly four hours of deliberation, the jury of 12 white men acquitted him. It was a new experience with Southern justice for the Kings. Mrs. King broke down into tears of joy and disbelief when the verdict was announced.

Later that year Dr. King had another brush with the law. Dr. King and 51 others were arrested during a sit-in in an Atlanta department store. The mayor of Atlanta managed to have the charges against the demonstrators dropped. But the judge decided that Dr. King's participation in a sit-in violated a 12-month parole. The parole was the result of a traffic conviction on a charge of driving in Georgia with an Alabama license. Dr. King was sentenced to four months of hard labor; no bail was allowed. He was handcuffed and taken to Reidsville State Prison to serve his sentence.

As Dr. King sat in solitary confinement, an Atlanta newspaper was calling his sentence a racial injustice. The U.S. Justice Department was pressuring President Eisenhower to publicly condemn the court's action and to call upon the Attorney General to apply for Dr. King's release. But the President did nothing. Vice-President Richard Nixon had no comment on the President's inaction.

It was October 1960 and Vice-President Nixon and Sen. John F. Kennedy were hotly contending for the Presidency of the United States. The Kennedy camp acted at once in Dr. King's behalf. Mr. Robert Kennedy, the Senator's brother and his campaign manager, called the judge and asked whether or not Dr. King had a constitutional right to bail. The candidate himself called Mrs. King and offered his sympathy and said that he would do all he could to help. The next day the judge granted Dr. King the right to bail and he was freed.

This action on the part of the Kennedys is believed to have had a very strong influence on the outcome of the election.

When President Kennedy was inaugurated, Dr. King thought he saw a supporter in the White House. He urged President Kennedy to issue a presidential order banning segregation in public facilities. He called upon the President to appoint a Secretary of Integration and to ask Congress for a Marshall Plan for America. "The President has proposed a ten-year plan to put a man on the moon. But we do not yet have a plan to put a Negro in the Alabama state legislature," said Dr. King.

During the first year or so of his administration Dr.

King found President Kennedy committed only to token integration. The new President seemed to be keenly aware of how slim his victory at the polls had been. He was feeling around for popular support of his policies. During this period President Kennedy did put the muscle of the Presidency behind Negro voters and job-hunters. In 1963 he emerged as a more active supporter of civil rights for the Negro.

While the President gathered support, CORE acted. This time the thrust was centered on the integration of interstate buses and the restroom and restaurants in the bus stations. On May 4, 1961, 13 Negroes and whites left Washington to take an integrated bus ride through the South. Through Virginia, North Carolina, and Georgia they traveled with no trouble. But when they reached Anniston, Ala., terrorists bombed and burned the bus. The Freedom Riders, as they were called, took another bus for Birmingham. When they arrived in Birmingham later that same day they were attacked and beaten by a mob. Now SNCC moved in to take up the campaign. A group of students took a bus for Montgomery on May 20. When they arrived in Montgomery, they were attacked by another mob.

The violence became so intense and open that Attorney General Robert Kennedy sent 400 U.S. marshals to Montgomery to maintain order. Dr. King flew to Montgomery to calm the outraged Negroes. On the evening of May 21, Dr. King held a mass meeting in Montgomery's First Baptist Church. As the meeting proceeded, a mob of white segregationists gathered outside the church. Standing between the 1,000 Negroes in the church and the mob was a squad of U.S. marshals and a few Montgomery city policemen. Someone in the mob shouted, "We want to integrate, too. Let us at them." Then a barrage of bottles and bricks was rained on the church. The marshals countered with tear gas. A battle raged for most of the night.

Inside the church the Negroes linked arms and sang the marching song of the civil rights movement, "We Shall Overcome."

We are not afraid . . . We are not afraid . . . We

are not afraid today . . . Oh, deep in my heart, I do believe . . . We shall overcome someday.

The Governor of Alabama sent national guardsmen to the church and declared martial law in Montgomery. The mob was dispersed and Dr. King and the others were given military escort to their homes.

Under CORE, SCLC, and SNCC leadership, the Freedom Rides continued with armed military protection including reconnaissance planes and helicopters. In three months the Interstate Commerce Commission reaffirmed its original ruling that segregation on buses and in bus stations was unlawful.

Up to this time Dr. King had never initiated a campaign. The Montgomery bus boycott, the sit-ins, and the freedom rides had all been started by others. He had moved in later to lead them. Now, with SCLC organized into an effective and strong civil rights group, the time came for him to initiate action.

When on December 12, 1961, 12 Freedom Riders were arrested in Albany, Ga., he thought he saw the opportunity and the place. At the invitation of civil rights leaders in Albany, Dr. King and his aides moved into the city and planned what would be the civil rights movement's first mass protest demonstration. The campaign would bring all the resources of the Negro community face to face with the city's total social and economic structure.

For a year Albany's Negroes, with Dr. King leading the way, marched on city hall, staged sit-ins in libraries and bowling alleys, and held prayer vigils on downtown streets. One thousand of the demonstrators went to jail. They were charged with illegal assembly, unlawful parades, and disturbing the peace. The chief of police saw to it that all demonstrators were handled with great care as they were taken off to jail. The nation found no brutality to be horrified at. The Federal Government did not intervene.

When Dr. King was jailed, he vowed to remain in jail until Albany saw fit to give the Negroes justice. He demanded that all public facilities be integrated, that Negro policemen and firemen be hired, that Negroes be allowed to participate fully in the life of Albany.

When Dr. King was misled into believing that he had won, he allowed himself to be bailed out of jail. Later he said, "I'm sorry I was bailed out. I didn't understand what was happening. We thought victory was won, but it was a hoax. We lost an initiative and we never regained it." Negroes won nothing in Albany. Albany remained segregated. It was not until the Civil Rights Bill of 1964 that even token integration came to Albany, Georgia.

Dr. King admitted that he had "jumped too far, too soon, and with improper preparation." He returned to Atlanta.

The defeat in Albany was the darkest hour yet for nonviolent direct action and its active, dynamic leader.

Chapter IX

Birmingham: A Matter Of Conscience

"Whites Only" signs were as plentiful in Birmingham, Ala., in early spring of 1963 as blossoms on a row of magnolia trees. The city was a perfect target for Negro demonstrations for integration, for equal treatment, for freedom.

Birmingham refused to allow Negro children to attend white schools. Negroes could not worship in white churches, drink at white water fountains, or eat at white restaurants. Negroes were born and died in colored hospitals.

A federal court ordered the city to integrate its parks in 1962. Rather than obey the order, the city closed all of its parks. Birmingham had given up its professional baseball team, too. The city preferred having no team at all to one that would play teams with some colored players. And there were so many unsolved bombings of Negro churches and homes that some people nicknamed the city Bombingham.

Martin Luther King, Jr. called Birmingham "the most thoroughly segregated big city in the U.S." Not long after his defeat in Albany, Ga., Dr. King began planning his attack on Birmingham's segregation.

He had made mistakes in Albany. He knew that. But he had learned from his mistakes. In Albany Dr. King and his followers had attacked segregation in general. Their protest wasn't aimed at a particular kind of segregation such as segregated schools. They didn't have a clear-cut target.

Dr. King decided that the Birmingham demonstrations had to be different. He knew that Birmingham Negroes had more power at the cash register than at the ballot box. Most of the city's Negroes couldn't vote. But they all shopped in Birmingham's stores.

If every Negro boycotted the stores, the businessmen

couldn't afford to keep lunch counters and restaurants segregated. Negro customers could mean the difference between a store making or losing money.

So Dr. King and Rev. Fred Shuttlesworth, a Birmingham civil rights leader, began to plan their strategy. They called their plan Project C. The C stood for the confrontation they would have with segregation in Birmingham.

A year earlier a group organized by Shuttlesworth and Miles College students had led a Negro boycott of several stores owned by white merchants. It was effective. Business fell off sharply and the businessmen agreed to talk to the Negro leaders.

But any progress was blocked by Eugene "Bull" Connor, the city's Commissioner of Public Safety. Connor was a firm segregationist, and some people claimed he threatened merchants who were willing to take down "colored" and "white" signs. Whatever the reasons, the signs did not come down in 1962.

Dr. King was determined that Project C would bring down the signs. Negroes would be able to eat next to white people in Birmingham before he would end the project.

Local elections delayed the start of the demonstrations. The city was governed by three commissioners, one of whom was Bull Connor. On March 5, 1963, Birmingham would elect its first mayor. Connor was a leading candidate. Although his chief opponents were also segregationists, they were much more moderate than Connor.

Negative reaction by white people to a series of Negro demonstrations during the political campaign, Dr. King feared, might help Connor win the election. Dr. King decided to wait, although he still hoped to organize a massive boycott before Easter Sunday, April 14. The demonstrations, he told his staff, would begin two weeks after the election.

But Dr. King had to postpone the demonstrations again. None of the candidates won a majority of the vote in March. A runoff election between the two top candidates, Lt. Gov. Albert Boutwell and Bull Connor, was scheduled for April 2.

If the demonstrations were going to have an effect on Easter shopping, they had to begin soon. Dr. King knew, however, that he couldn't risk doing anything that might help Connor win the election. So he ordered all of his Southern Christian Leadership Conference staff to leave Birmingham.

Dr. King returned to the city on Wednesday, April 3. The front-page headline in the *Birmingham News* that day read, "New Day Dawns for Birmingham."

The headline was even more accurate than the newspaper could have intended. The editors saw a new day because Albert Boutwell had defeated Bull Connor. But the demonstrations that Dr. King was about to begin were the real beginning of a new day for Birmingham.

Dr. King promised that the demonstrations would go on until "Pharaoh lets God's people go." That time would come, he said, when Negroes would be given equal job opportunities, when Negroes would be free to eat at white lunch counters and restaurants, and when the city would set up a biracial commission to end segregation.

Most white Birmingham residents believed Dr. King had no right to come into the city and demand anything. They denounced him. Many white Americans in other parts of the country, including Attorney General Robert Kennedy and Evangelist Billy Graham, questioned the timing of Dr. King's protest. They believed a cooling-off period was needed after Bull Connor's narrow defeat.

Even more disappointing to Dr. King was the reaction among Birmingham's Negroes. Like many whites, they believed the city would be a different place without Bull Connor. His defeat, they felt, was a major victory. They thought the new Mayor should be given a chance before anyone started demonstrations.

Much of the Negro community's cool reception to Dr. King's speech was the result of hurt pride. Dr. King had not consulted all of the local Negro leadership before he announced his plans for the Birmingham campaign. These people felt left out. Their first reaction was to ignore Dr. King.

Dr. King was in a dangerous situation. He had committed himself in a public speech. If he failed to rally Negro support, after his Albany defeat, he would lose his effectiveness as a leader. And if he failed, the nonviolent movement would probably fail with him.

The demonstrations began on a small scale. Dr. King had learned in Albany that it is important for a campaign to start quietly and gradually build to a climax. At first there were a few sit-ins at lunch counters and a few arrests.

During those first days Dr. King tried to rally the support of Birmingham's Negro leadership. Without these people his plan would wither and die like a rose in the desert. He went from meeting to meeting, explaining that the political situation had forced him to keep Project C secret. To those who thought Dr. King's timing was poor, he pointed out that the demonstrations had already been postponed twice.

Indirectly and unintentionally, Dr. King was probably helped most of all by Bull Connor. Connor and the other commissioners had filed a legal suit claiming they had a right to remain in office until their terms expired in 1965. If they won, they would be in power for two more years. Birmingham Negroes certainly did not want that.

Gradually Dr. King's plan picked up support. If his opponents were not convinced that the plan was good or the timing appropriate, they remained quiet. Dr. King met secretly with his top aides. The early stages of the Birmingham campaign had been wrapped in secrecy. Suspecting that their phones would be tapped, Dr. King and his staff used code names during telephone conversations. Dr. King was "J.F.K.," Ralph Abernathy was "Dean Rusk," Fred Shuttlesworth was "Bull," and businessman John Drew was "Pope John." They called the demonstrators "baptismal candidates."

Dr. King was ready to move into the streets. On Saturday, April 6, a group of carefully selected demonstrators marched on City Hall. Two by two, they marched silently through the streets of Birmingham.

A row of Birmingham policemen blocked the marchers' path about three blocks from City Hall.

Both sides were calm and polite. The police ordered the marchers to disperse. They refused. Quietly, they were escorted into police wagons.

Each day the demonstrations grew bigger. Downtown stores began to feel the pinch of an almost total Negro boycott. Greater numbers of people were arrested as Negroes led a voter registration march. Sit-ins at lunch counters and at the library, and kneel-ins at white churches also led to arrest and jail.

The police remained nonviolent. Bull Connor had also learned from the Albany demonstrations. He was trying to handle nonviolent demonstrations with nonviolent methods.

Connor then moved to end the demonstrations through the local courts. On April 10 a court injunction ordered the demonstrations to stop. Before they could begin again, the court said, Dr. King and his followers would have to appear in court and argue their right to demonstrate.

Bull Connor was convinced he had won. Dr. King had never disobeyed a court order.

For several months Dr. King and his staff had discussed the possibility of civil disobedience. That is, they considered willfully disobeying the law. They knew that someday a local court would forbid them to demonstrate. They had prayed for guidance and they had decided they would disobey such an order.

Dr. King believed the court was using its power to maintain an unjust system of segregation. A man is required to obey a law, Dr. King told his followers, only when the law is just and right. A just law, he said, "squares with the moral law, or the law of God." But if a man's conscience tells him that a human law violates the law of God, Dr. King said, he should disobey the law.

So, on Good Friday, Dr. King and Ralph Abernathy dressed in gray work shirts and blue jeans and led about 40 demonstrators into the street. They knew they would be arrested. And they knew they might not be able to bail themselves out of jail because all of the bail funds available to them had already been used up.

The march began at the Sixth Avenue Zion Hill

Church. Slowly, the marchers headed for the city's downtown section. A thousand Negroes lined the streets singing "We Shall Overcome" as the marchers approached. They cheered as the group passed by chanting "Freedom has come to Birmingham!" Some dropped to their knees in silent prayer.

Then, after eight blocks, the march was over. Bull Connor had seen enough. "Don't let them go any farther," he shouted. Dr. King, Reverend Abernathy, and 53 demonstrators were arrested.

Dr. King was separated from the others in jail. He was not allowed to make any phone calls or talk to anyone. He had no way of knowing what was happening in the city. He worried about the movement, about the other demonstrators, about the morale of Birmingham's Negroes.

And he worried about his wife and children. Only two weeks before, his wife had given birth to their fourth child. He had always been able to call her after an arrest to tell her he was safe. And she had always given him the strength to carry on.

At her home in Atlanta, Mrs. King was upset. She knew her husband had been arrested. But why hadn't he called? Had he been injured—or killed?

Remembering the call John Kennedy had made to her during the 1960 presidential campaign, she decided to call him. She was unable to reach him. A few minutes later Attorney General Robert Kennedy called her. He promised to find out the situation in Birmingham. Within a few hours, he assured her that her husband was safe.

The following morning President Kennedy called Mrs. King. He had talked to officials in Birmingham, he said, and had arranged to have Dr. King call home. He told her that he had sent the FBI to Birmingham to keep a check on Dr. King's safety.

While he was in jail, Dr. King was told that he had been severely criticized by a group of Birmingham's white religious leaders. They called him an intruder, an outsider who had come to Birmingham to stir up trouble. They urged "our own Negro community to withdraw support" from Dr. King's "unwise and untimely" movement.

Sitting in his cell, he wrote a letter to his critics. In his famous "Letter from a Birmingham Jail," he outlined the philosophy behind the nonviolent movement and the civil rights struggle. He wrote on any scrap of paper he could get hold of, even in the margins of old newspapers. Then, in bits and pieces, an aide smuggled the letter out of the jail.

In the letter, addressed to "My Dear Fellow Clergymen," he described what it was like to be a Negro in America. He explained why the Negro couldn't wait for equality any longer. He said that a Negro father has to tell his children that they can't go to places advertised on television for white children. Whites call him nigger or boy in front of his family. Everywhere he turns, the Negro is humiliated and made to feel inferior, wrote Dr. King.

"I guess it is easy," Dr. King wrote to the clergymen, "for those who have never felt the stinging darts of segregaton to say 'wait.' "

Then Dr. King received some good news. Singer Harry Belafonte had raised $50,000 for bail bonds. If more was needed, Belafonte promised to raise it.

Eight days after they were arrested, Dr. King and Ralph Abernathy posted bond. Dr. King was anxious to begin new demonstrations.

About 500 demonstrators had been arrested up to that point. Most of them were adults. Dr. King was convinced that the movement had to attract the city's Negro students to be successful. He wanted to involve them in the struggle; to show the youngsters that they had a stake in the future of the movement.

Most whites and many Negroes sharply criticized Dr. King for risking children's lives in the demonstrations. But the Birmingham children's crusade proved to be one of the most important events in the history of the civil rights movement in the United States.

Students were invited to attend mass meetings at churches after school. Youngsters were taught what nonviolence was all about at formal training sessions. By May 2 the Negro children of Birmingham were ready to march.

More than 1,000 students, most of them teen-agers,

marched on that muggy Thursday afternoon. They left
the Sixteenth St. Baptist Church in small groups. While
police were arresting one group, another would appear
on the other side of the street. Many of the students
reached downtown before they were arrested. Birmingham policemen arrested 1,000 people that afternoon.
Most of those arrested sang as they were driven off to
jail.

An even larger group of marchers left the church
the next day. "We want freedom," they chanted, "We
want freedom." A long line of policemen blocked their
path. A police captain ordered them to stop.

"We want freedom," was their answer. The students
kept on marching. Furious, Bull Connor ordered
fire engines at the scene to turn their high-powered
hoses on the marchers.

The teen-agers remembered Dr. King's philosophy
of nonviolence. They sat on the pavement, some with
their hands on their heads. Crushing streams of water
flattened youngsters against the sidewalk. Some tried
to get up and were knocked down. Many lay bleeding
on the cement.

Across the street, in Kelly Ingram Park, about 1,500
adult Negroes were horrified at the brutal treatment of
their children. They shouted threats. They began to
throw rocks, then bottles and bricks at Connor's men.
A deputy sheriff who was struck by a rock shouted,
"Those black apes!"

Connor was ready for trouble. At his command, five
police dogs were brought out to the street. The dogs
nipped at the ankles of people in the crowd, and
ripped open trousers.

"Look at 'em run," Connor said, "look at those niggers run."

But they didn't run far. Most of the demonstrators
stood their ground. The snarling dogs lunged at the
crowd. Gradually the dogs drove the crowd back to
the church.

By this time an angry mob of Negroes was forming
at the scene. People who hadn't been part of Dr. King's
demonstrations appeared from side streets. Some of
them carried knives, bottles, and guns.

A white mob formed, too. Before long both sides were hurling rocks and bottles at each other.

Rev. Fred Shuttlesworth tried to calm the rioters. Standing on the church steps, he pleaded with them to stop fighting. Suddenly a blast of water slammed him against a brick wall. Shuttlesworth had to be taken to a hospital in an ambulance for treatment of a chest injury.

When Connor was told later, he said, "I waited a week down here to see that and then I missed it. I wish it had been a hearse."

Two hours after Bull Connor ordered the hoses turned on the marchers, the battle was over. There was an uneasy peace in Birmingham that night.

Alabama's Governor George Wallace sent 600 state police into the city to relieve Connor's men. Attorney General Kennedy tried to arrange a compromise between Negro leaders and the city's new mayor. He failed.

Dr. King spoke to 1,000 people at a church meeting that night. "The eyes of the world are on Birmingham," he said. "We're going on in spite of dogs and fire hoses. We've gone too far to turn back."

He was right. The eyes of the world *were* on Birmingham. That night, television news programs carried scenes of police dogs growling at children and women sprawled helpless under the force of a fire hose. Newspapers and magazines printed scores of pictures, especially one that showed two policemen holding a woman on the ground. One of the men had a knee jammed against her throat.

The pictures and stories of what had happened in Birmingham shocked America and the rest of the world. Many citizens of Birmingham, too, were disturbed by the way Connor had dealt with the demonstrators. A sizable number of white residents believed the Negroes deserved a better life. They had demonstrated that belief by not electing Bull Connor as their mayor.

Even some people who were strong segregationists wanted to find a peaceful solution to the demonstrations. They worried about what police dogs and fire hoses would do to the city's image. And businessmen who were losing money wanted to find a way to end the Negro boycott of their stores.

President Kennedy sent two of his top assistants to Birmingham to begin a series of meetings between Negro and white leaders. But Dr. King had no intention of taking the pressure off Birmingham officials. The demonstrations continued. "If the white power structure of this city will meet some of our minimum demands," he said, "we will consider calling off the demonstrations, but we want promises, plus action."

He repeated his demands: (1) desegregate all public facilities in local stores; (2) give Negroes equal job opportunities; (3) drop all charges against the 2,500 demonstrators who had been arrested; (4) set up a biracial committee to reopen the city parks and other facilities that had been closed to avoid integration.

After a week of secret negotiations the two sides arrived at a truce. The businessmen agreed to meet Dr. King's demands. On Friday, May 10, the agreement was announced. America breathed a sigh of relief. The Birmingham crisis seemed over.

Some of Birmingham's segregationists, however, felt the businessmen had betrayed them. Raging with anger, they met at a Ku Klux Klan meeting Saturday night. Shortly after the meeting, an explosion rocked the home of Dr. King's brother, the Rev. A. D. King. Reverend King and his wife led their five children to safety just in time. A second dynamite bomb blasted the house.

Another bomb ripped through the Gaston Motel that night. If Dr. King had been in his headquarters in Room 30, he would have been seriously injured or killed by the explosion. But he had returned to Atlanta on Saturday.

The Birmingham truce had been shattered. Thousands of angry Negroes poured into the streets. They flung stones, bottles, bricks. They hurled torches at white men's stores. Rioters fought off firemen who tried to put out the fires. Only a few days before, these same firemen had aimed their hoses at Negro children. The rioters hadn't forgotten. "White men, we'll kill you!" they screamed.

Dr. King's brother called him in Atlanta. Horrified by the situation in Birmingham, Dr. King rushed back to the city.

The sun rose that Sunday morning on a tense but quiet Mother's Day in Birmingham. About 250 state troopers had been called into the city. The rioters had returned to their homes.

That night President Kennedy went on television to warn white and black extremists. The Federal Government intended to protect the agreement worked out by the city's businessmen and Negro leaders. As a safety precaution the President ordered 3,000 federal troops to military bases near Birmingham. If necessary, he said, he would also federalize the Alabama National Guard to keep peace in Birmingham.

Dr. King knew that the people who had bombed his brother's house and the motel had wanted the Negroes to riot. They had hoped a bloody, destructive riot would force the white businessmen to pull out of their agreement.

The nonviolent movement would be destroyed if Negroes rioted every time they were provoked by segregationists. Malcolm X, the Negro racist leader of the Black Muslims, was encouraged by the Saturday night riot. He hoped the nonviolent movement would die because he thought it was ineffective. "The lesson of Birmingham is that the Negroes have lost their fear of the white man's reprisals and will react with violence, if provoked," Malcolm X said.

Dr. King was determined that such rioting would not happen in Birmingham again. He began what was called a "poolroom pilgrimage." He went to the people who had rioted.

He walked into barrooms, pool halls—wherever he could find people to talk to. He interrupted their pool games and they listened as he explained his gospel of nonviolence. There would probably be more attempts to drive the Negroes to violence, Dr. King warned. If Birmingham's Negroes were going to make any progress, he told them, they had to avoid falling into the segregationists' trap of violence.

"Violence is immoral," he said, "but not only that—violence is impractical."

On May 20 segregationists set another trap. The Board of Education announced that more than 1,000 student demonstrators had been either expelled or suspended from school.

Many Negroes, even Dr. King's close followers, were enraged. They wanted to urge all of the city's Negro students to boycott the schools. And they wanted to plan new demonstrations in the streets.

But Dr. King discouraged them. The city was so tense that a school boycott and more marches would probably lead to more violence. So Dr. King convinced Birmingham's Negro leaders to take their argument with the school board to court.

A local judge upheld the school board's decision. Again there was pressure for more demonstrations. But an appeals court judge overruled the first judge—and strongly condemned the school board for its decision. The student demonstrators were allowed to go back to school.

Birmingham's Negro community rejoiced at a mass meeting that night. There was new hope in their voices as they sang the now familiar words: "Deep in my heart, I do believe, we shall overcome someday."

The next day brought even more encouraging news. The Alabama Supreme Court ruled that Eugene (Bull) Connor and the other commissioners did not have the right to remain in office for an additional two years. The election results were final. Bull Connor was no longer in power in Birmingham.

The hope that was born in Birmingham spread across the nation. In more than 800 cities and towns Negroes began to demonstrate for the rights they had been denied. Discrimination against the Negro was not confined to the South—and the civil rights struggle became a national movement.

Dr. King became world famous and a national leader. After he left Birmingham he spoke in several major cities. In Chicago 10,000 people turned out to hear him speak. In Los Angeles 25,000 people listened to his pleas for equality. In Detroit he led 125,000 people in a peaceful Freedom Walk. The Negro's demand echoed from coast to coast: "Freedom Now!"

President Kennedy heard that demand. During his first two years in office he had moved cautiously on the civil rights issue. But the events in Birmingham had helped to create what Dr. King described as "a new Kennedy."

On June 11, 1963, President Kennedy asked Congress to pass the most far-reaching civil rights legislation ever proposed by a President. The bill called for Negro voting rights, employment opportunities, and the end of segregation in all public facilities.

In a dramatic address the President said, "One hundred years of delay have passed since President Lincoln freed the slaves, yet their heirs, their grandsons, are not fully free. They are not yet freed from the bonds of injustice; they are not yet freed from social and economic oppression. And this nation, for all its hopes and its boasts, will not be fully free until all its citizens are free."

Six weeks of demonstrations in Birmingham had stirred the nation's conscience. The city's brutal treatment of the Negro demonstrators had dramatized the evils of segregation. And it had convinced many people that it was time for the Negroes to achieve equality.

"Our judgment of Bull Connor should not be too harsh," President Kennedy told Dr. King. "The civil rights movement owes Bull Connor as much as it owes Abraham Lincoln."

Chapter X

Washington:
'I Have A Dream . . .'

"It's just like they were getting ready for D-Day in
Normandy," said one official in Washington, D.C.

In a sense, he was right. The March on Washington
for Jobs and Freedom in August 1963 was the largest
civil rights rally in American history. And the leaders
of the march planned it as carefully as generals plan a
major invasion.

The idea for the march was first proposed in January
by two Negro leaders, Bayard Rustin and Norman Hill,
and a white friend, Tom Kahn. In a letter to A. Phillip
Randolph, the only Negro member of the Executive
Council of the AFL-CIO labor union, they suggested a
mass march on Washington, D.C. It would be a dramatic
way of helping Negroes to get jobs, they said.

The 74-year-old Randolph thought it was a good
idea. On May 4, in the midst of the Birmingham demonstrations, Mr. Randolph told a reporter, "We're going
to march on Washington."

Marches in the nation's capital were nothing new to
the Negro labor leader. In 1941 he planned a mass
march on Washington to protest the lack of jobs for Negroes in wartime industry. President Roosevelt called
him to the White House and asked him to cancel the
march. Mr. Randolph refused. The President then agreed
to create the Fair Employment Practices Commission,
an important step towards forbidding racial discrimination in industry The march was called off.

Then, in 1948, Mr. Randolph threatened that Negroes
would not register for the draft unless segregation was
abolished in the armed forces. Within a short time
President Harry S. Truman integrated all U.S. military
bases and units.

In 1957 Mr. Randolph led 20,000 people to Washington to mark the third anniversary of the Supreme

Court's order to end segregation in public schools. This time it was President Dwight D. Eisenhower who was urged by the marchers to "speak out" for civil rights.

The following year, 1958, Mr. Randolph organized a Youth March in Washington. Nearly 10,000 Negro and white students marched to the Lincoln Memorial to protest racial inequality.

But the March for Jobs and Freedom would be the biggest march Washington had ever seen. The time was right.

The Birmingham demonstrations had ripped open the nation's conscience. Birmingham had given hope to Negroes who had resigned themselves to a life of oppression. For America's Negroes the battle of Birmingham stimulated the civil rights movement like a sudden charge of electricity.

Dr. King and the nation's other Negro leaders joined Mr. Randolph in his call for a march on Washington. All of the important Negro organizations—the National Association for the Advancement of Colored People (NAACP), the Congress of Racial Equality (CORE), the Student Nonviolent Coordinating Committee (SNCC), the Urban League, and Dr. King's own Southern Christian Leadership Conference—all planned for the march.

Dr. King suggested that the march have a broader goal than employment. The marchers' goal should include all Negro rights, he said. The other leaders agreed, and the march took on a wider national meaning.

While the Negro leaders talked and planned, they appealed to white leaders to join the march. Their struggle was one of justice against injustice, not black against white. The march would be more effective, they believed, if white people participated. Walter Reuther, President of the powerful United Auto Workers, and representatives of the Catholic, Jewish, and Protestant faiths soon joined. Religious leaders all across the nation urged their congregations to support the march. Labor unions contributed $50,000 as well as volunteering men and women to march. Mayors in several big cities gave employees the day off to march on Washington.

The more people involved, the greater the danger that the march would explode into a riot. Every precaution was taken to make sure that the march would be completely peaceful, lawful, and nonviolent.

Official agencies, from the Washington Police Department to the U.S. Army, sat in on planning sessions. Without civilian and military policemen to direct and redirect cars and buses, the march would become clogged in a fantastic traffic jam.

Marchers were asked to travel to Washington by bus or train to reduce the threat of traffic tie-ups. They were also asked to leave any children under 14 at home.

It would be a long, hot day for the marchers. Fire hydrants along the route were installed with bubbler devices, turning them into drinking fountains. Spaces were reserved for large trucks to move into the area to sell sandwiches and soft drinks.

There were 22 first aid stations, too. Blisters, sunstroke, heart attacks, even emergency surgery would be handled along the march route. And in case of trouble there were policeman and soldiers—more than 2,000 policemen and 2,000 National Guardsmen. Nearby, 4,000 Army and Marine troops were ready if needed. The march leaders themselves had organized 2,000 marshals to keep things calm and quiet.

Bayard Rustin spoke for all of the planners when he said, "Our aim is to get each marcher to understand fully the significance of why he is there. We are asking each person to be a marshal of himself, since anybody who turns to violence will be a traitor to our cause."

The marchers started arriving in Washington. Carpenters were still building platforms for TV cameras at the Lincoln Memorial the night before the march when the first few Negroes arrived.

Washington the next morning was clear and cool. Although it was a Wednesday morning, the city had a Sunday atmosphere. There was no early morning rush-hour traffic. The people who drove into Washington to work every morning had turned the city over to the marchers for the day.

By 9:30 a.m. 40,000 people had assembled at the Washington Monument, where the march would start at

11:30. An hour before the march was due to begin, 90,000 people were there.

Buses and trains still streamed into Washington from every part of the country. They came from places such as New York, Jacksonville, Chicago, Birmingham, and Detroit. From small town and big city, men and women came to march for freedom.

They were quiet. When they raised their voices, it was to sing. Teen-agers from the Deep South, most of whom had been arrested at least once in demonstrations, sang as they piled off their Freedom Special train. Adult marchers caught their spirit and joined in. They sang "Freedom, Freedom!," "Good News, Freedom Comin'," and their battle hymn, "We Shall Overcome."

And they prayed. "Help us, O Lord," they prayed, "not to disgrace ourselves this day. Help us to make this a proud day."

By 11:20 a.m. the marchers were impatient. The Kenilworth Knights, a Washington drum and bugle corps dressed in green berets, yellow silk blazers, and green trousers, suddenly and without warning began to march towards the Lincoln Memorial. Many of the marchers followed them.

"My God," cried Rustin, "they're going. We're supposed to be leading them." He rounded up the other leaders of the march and they set out with a second wave of people.

The first group of marchers chanted "Freedom—Freedom—Freedom," setting a cadence for the other marchers to follow. Dr. King smiled about the spontaneous beginning of the march. A "revolution," he told a companion, "is supposed to be unpredictable."

Only one of the leaders who had planned the march was not in Washington. James Farmer, National Director of CORE, was in a Louisiana jail with a group of demonstrators. One of his assistants took his place in the march.

Wave after wave of marchers left the Washington Monument. Less than a mile away, at the Lincoln Memorial, nearly 250,000 people waited for the speeches to begin. No one had foreseen such a large turnout.

On the sidelines George Lincoln Rockwell and 50

members of his American Nazi Party watched. Police prevented them from interfering with the marchers, but Rockwell's uniformed followers shouted at and booed the marchers. Before he led his frustrated storm troopers away, Rockwell muttered, "I can't stand niggers. I can't stand to hear 'We Shall Overcome.' "

The huge crowd waited quietly while the leaders of the march met with President Kennedy at the White House. While they waited for the leaders to return to the Lincoln Memorial, the crowd listened to a string of singers and Hollywood actors that included Harry Belafonte, Joan Baez, Paul Newman, Peter-Paul-and-Mary, Charlton Heston, Odetta, and Bob Dylan.

The conversation at the White House lasted for 75 minutes. The leaders talked with the President about the prospects for passage of his civil rights bill. And they told President Kennedy—as they had told some of Congress' most powerful leaders that morning—that even more legislation was needed.

They asked the President for a federal fair employment practices commission, and power for the Justice Department to step into civil rights disputes on the state and local level. After his conference with the march leaders, President Kennedy said, "One cannot help but be impressed with the quiet dignity that characterizes the thousands who have gathered in the nation's capital from across the country to demonstrate their faith and confidence in our democratic form of government."

And the President urged the nation to speed up its efforts to guarantee equal rights for all citizens—in education, jobs, and voting.

The leaders returned to the Lincoln Memorial. One by one they stepped before the microphones and TV cameras and spoke to the marchers and to the world.

It was a hot 83 degrees. The marchers were tired. Some took off their shoes and cooled their feet in the pools near the monument. Some looked for a bit of shade under the green branches of a tree. They listened to the speakers. They applauded. Mr. Randolph looked to the future. "We are the advance guard of a massive moral revolution," he told the marchers. "We here today are only the first wave."

Urban League director Whitney Young told the crowd that the march on Washington was not enough. If they were going to win the civil rights struggle, he said, the marchers would have to go home and walk "together to the PTA meetings—the libraries—the decision-making meetings—the schools and colleges—the voter registration booths."

Floyd McKissick read a speech written by the jailed James Farmer. "We will not stop," he said, "until the dogs stop biting us in the South and the rats stop biting us in the North."

Some of the marchers, exhausted after all-night bus rides to Washington and hours of standing and walking, began to leave the Lincoln Memorial. For those who stayed, the heat seemed to be getting worse. But those who left missed two highlights of the day.

Singer Mahalia Jackson took her turn before the microphones. Her voiced echoed across centuries of oppression as she sang the sorrowful spiritual, "I've Been 'Buked and I've Been Scorned." The marchers sobbed and wiped tears from their faces as they listened to the gospel singer, who herself was close to tears.

Miss Jackson's stirring performance readied the crowd for the words of the next speaker. As they saw him approach the platform, the crowd burst into such an uproar that they drowned out his introduction.

As Martin Luther King, Jr. began to speak, the hush of a cathedral fell over the crowd. Like a well-tuned church bell, his voice pealed the marchers' message across the huge mall between the Lincoln Memorial and the Washington Monument.

"I have a dream," he cried.

The crowd roared. "Tell us!"

"I have a dream—that the sons of former slaves and the sons of former slave owners will be able to sit together at the table of brotherhood."

"Yes! Yes! I see it!" roared the crowds.

"I have a dream that my four little children will one day live in a nation where they will not be judged by the color of their skin, but by the content of their character."

"Oh, yes! Dream on! Dream!" cried the crowd.

Then it was over. It was the emotional peak of the day. Dr. King's words summarized the centuries of anguish and injustice, but also described a world of the future in which people of all races would be truly free. The crowd slowly moved away from the Lincoln Memorial. Some hummed the freedom songs they had sung earlier. Most were silent, thinking about a day that was now history, thinking about what the success of the huge march might mean.

Senator Hubert Humphrey said, "All this probably hasn't changed any votes on the civil rights bill—but it's a good thing for Washington and the nation and the world."

But what about the marchers themselves? Why had they come to Washington—and what did they hope to achieve?

A Negro woman from Los Angeles explained why she had made the trip. "You can never know," she told a white marcher, "what it's like to be a Negro. No matter how you try, you can't imagine going into a hamburger shop with your children and being told, 'We don't serve niggers here.' "

The wife of a Negro truck driver from Birmingham went to Washington even though she had to make many sacrifices to pay for her $8 bus ticket. "If I ever had any doubts before," she said, "they're gone now. When I get back home I'm going to follow this on out. I've followed it this far. When I get back there tomorrow I'm going to do whatever needs to be done—I don't care if it's picketing or marching or sitting-in or what. I'm ready to do it."

So they went home—determined that the march on Washington would make a difference. And there were reasons to hope that it would.

White churchmen for the first time had enthusiastically and effectively entered the civil rights struggle. Largely because of their clergy's participation, about 60,000 white people joined the march. Many of them had carried signs reading: "We march together—Catholics, Jews, Protestants—for dignity and brotherhood of all men under God. NOW!"

White people in the march, Floyd McKissick said, marked "the end of the Negro protest and the beginning of the American protest."

Newspaper and television stories the next day were full of praise for the march, the marchers, and Dr. King. A Negro taxi driver in New York summed up what people all over the world felt. "It was wonderful," he said. "That Martin Luther King—he said a mouthful. It's still ringing in my ears."

On the day after the march, Dr. King returned to the Lincoln Memorial to be interviewed by a British television reporter. With the large white marble statue of Lincoln behind him, Dr. King said:

"The demonstration, I am certain, has already done a great deal to create a coalition of concern about the status of civil rights in this country. It has aroused the conscience of millions of people to work for this legislation." He also announced that day that the leaders of the march were beginning "a mass write-in campaign so that people in the tens of thousands will urge doubtful congressmen to pass" the civil rights bill.

The feeling of optimism, of good things about to happen, lasted less than three weeks.

On a September Sunday morning a bomb exploded in Birmingham that shook the entire nation. Birmingham was not expecting trouble that Sunday morning. Earlier in the week, when the city opened its schools to Negroes for the first time, many people feared there would be violence. But except for a few white protests the city had been quiet.

Sunday began normally as parents got their children ready for Sunday school. Like scores of other parents in Birmingham that morning, Claude Wesley drove his daughter to the church where she would attend her religious class. Mr. Wesley, principal of a Negro school, drove 14-year-old Cynthia to the Sixteenth Street Baptist Church. He let her off in front of the church and continued down the street. Two blocks away he stopped at a gas station. It was 9:22 a.m.

The morning calm was shattered by a ferocious explosion, a blast ripped through the brick walls and stained-glass windows of the church. Screams of pain and terror seared Mr. Wesley's heart. He ran toward the ruins of the church.

When he got there, his Cynthia and three other young Negro girls were dead.

More than 400 people had been in the church when the bomb exploded. Stunned, many badly injured, they staggered through the wreckage into the street.

"In church!" screamed one Negro woman. "My God, you're not even safe in church!"

The sound of the explosion drew hundreds of others to the scene. "Murderers!" cried a sobbing woman. A man, filled with hate, repeated: "Let me at them. I'll kill them—I'll kill them!"

Birmingham threatened to explode as passion-torn Negroes crowded into the street outside the church. Policemen tried to break up the crowd by firing shots into the air. Almost hysterical, the crowd threw shattered pieces of stained glass and brick at the policemen.

Negroes and whites fought on street corners all around the city. Young white men waved the Confederate flag and jeered young Negroes. Both sides threw rocks. There was chaos in the streets.

Police broke up one fight Sunday afternoon. The Negro youths ran away. A policeman ordered them to halt. They didn't. A shotgun blast made Johnny Robinson, 16, stop. He died before he arrived at the hospital.

In another corner of the city Jimmy Ware, 16, was giving his brother Virgil, 13, a ride home on his bicycle. Two young white boys, riding a motorbike, passed them. One of the white boys had a pistol. He fired twice. Virgil fell dead from the handlebars where he had been riding.

Dr. King was horrified at the news from Birmingham. He raced back to the city. His presence, along with the influence of leaders such as Reverend Shuttlesworth, prevented even more violence.

At the four girls' funeral, Dr. King said the youngsters were martyrs. "They have something to say to all of us," he said, "to ministers safe behind stained-glass windows, to politicians who feed their constituents the stale bread of hatred and the spoiled meat of racism. . . ."

The deaths of the six Birmingham children shattered the hope that the Washington march had created. Many began to demand immediate action. They pressured Dr. King to lead a full-scale attack on American society.

A group of Negro students wanted to declare a war of civil disobedience. They wanted to blockade airports, bus terminals, train stations, and city streets. They wanted to boycott stores, to go out on strike, and to stop paying taxes. In short, they wanted to immobilize America until something was done to help the Negro.

Dr. King rejected their plan because he believed that it would cause disunity among Negroes. Without the unity of all the various Negro groups with their different plans of action, Dr. King knew that the civil rights movement would fail. Gains that had already been made might be lost.

As Negro impatience grew in the fall of 1963, so did the white fear of Negro progress. A "white backlash" of bigotry came into the open. Public opinion polls showed that President Kennedy was losing popularity among white voters. And the civil rights bill still had not passed in Congress.

Dr. King expected resentment among Northern whites. "Demonstrations in such cities as New York and Chicago," he said, "aroused the ire of many persons in the North. But the Negro revolution has revealed to many persons in the North that they had more deep-seated prejudices than they realized."

Hatred seeped through the nation that autumn. It was contagious, Dr. King said, and it infected everything it touched. In this atmosphere on a bright November morning in Dallas, Tex., an assassin killed President John F. Kennedy.

Dr. King returned to Washington to attend the President's funeral. With kings, queens, and leaders of the world's great nations, he marched in the solemn funeral procession. Three months earlier he had marched in this same city with poor people, full of hope. Now he marched with some of the most powerful people in the world—filled with grief.

In the days following the assassination of President Kennedy, Dr. King again saw signs of hope. Louis Harris, the public opinion analyst, found that "the death of President Kennedy produced a profound change in the thinking of the American people; a massive rejection of extremism from either right or left, accompanied by an individual sense of guilt for not working for more tolerance toward others."

Grief-stricken Americans looked for ways to honor President Kennedy. Schools, bridges, airports, and streets were named for him. But his real monument would not come, Dr. King said, until America enlarged its "sense of humanity. . . ."

Chapter XI

Prize:
And Back
To The Valley

Yolanda (Yoki) Denise King was the proudest third grader in Atlanta as she stood before her class.

"There was a man named Alfred Nobel," she said. "He was a millionaire. And when he died, he said that he would like to have a Peace Prize. The man who made the most peace—he would get $54,600. There were three Negroes to win the Peace Prize. The first was Ralph Bunche in 1950. The second was Chief Albert J. Luthuli. The third was my daddy. And he won it in 1964."

The Nobel Peace Prize is one of the greatest honors that a man can receive. It is given to the organization or person who has done the most for the "furtherance of brotherhood among men."

If there is no one worthy of the award in a particular year, the Prize is not given. Among the earlier winners were President Theodore Roosevelt, President Woodrow Wilson, and the International Red Cross.

On October 14, 1964, Dr. King learned that he had won the Nobel Peace Prize. He was the 12th American to win the Prize, which is awarded by members of the Norwegian parliament.

"I am glad people of other nations," Dr. King said, "are concerned with our problems here."

He added, "I do not consider this merely an honor to me personally, but a tribute to the disciplined, wise restraint and majestic courage of gallant Negro and white persons of goodwill who have followed a nonviolent course in seeking to establish a reign of justice and a rule of love across this nation of ours." He announced that every penny of the $54,600 Prize would be used in the civil rights movement.

When Dr. King was told he had won the Nobel Peace Prize, he was in an Atlanta hospital bed. "I just kind of got run-down," he told reporters, so he had gone into the hospital for a checkup and "to get some rest."

He had reason to be tired. In the 11 months following President Kennedy's assassination in November 1963, Dr. King had led the civil rights movement into a string of Northern and Southern cities—Atlanta, Chicago, Cleveland.

He had begun slowly. He told people that the temporary slowdown in civil rights activity was "the inevitable pause that takes place in any movement to assess your gains, to determine your future course, and to put yourself in a better position for future leaps." Many of the people who had demonstrated with Dr. King didn't want to slow down. "I'm running into more and more bitterness because things haven't moved fast enough," he said.

In the spring of 1964, Dr. King made his next important move. The target for massive demonstrations was St. Augustine, Fla. The oldest city in the U.S., St. Augustine was celebrating its 400th anniversary. National attention was focused on the city.

Dr. King planned to take advantage of that attention to help end the city's total segregation. His campaign received some unexpected publicity in April when an arrested picketer turned out to be Mrs. Malcolm Peabody, mother of the Governor of Massachusetts. By May the campaign reached its peak while the nation watched.

St. Augustine presented Dr. King with problems that he had not faced in any other city. The city's policemen, for the most part, looked the other way during the demonstrations. That was part of the problem. White segregationists attacked the demonstrators as they held "wade-ins" at the city's Whites Only beaches. Armed with clubs, chains—even containers of acid—they mobbed the demonstrators. Many were injured. But the police did little to prevent the attacks.

Rabble-rousers from other parts of the nation flocked to St. Augustine to fight the Negro and white demonstrators. One of them, a California man, screamed out to. a mob: "I favor violence to preserve the white race any time, anyplace, anywhere. Now I grant you, some niggers are gonna get killed in the process, but when war's on that's what happens."

Dr. King pleaded for protection. He contacted President Johnson, telling him St. Augustine was "the most lawless community" he had ever seen.

But, Dr. King made clear, "we are determined. There will be no turning back."

Gov. Farris Bryant sent Florida state troopers into the city to put down a white brick-throwing mob. With the troopers in charge, most of the violence ended. Then, on June 11, Dr. King was arrested. He had gone to one of the best restaurants in the city and asked to be served. "We can't serve you here," the owner said, "we're not integrated."

"We will stand here," Dr. King said, "and hope that in the process that our conscious efforts will make this a better land."

The owner stood fast, too. "Negroes can only be served in the service area of the restaurant," he said. "Maids and chauffeurs of white visitors have been served that way in the past."

"Do you understand what this does to our dignity?" Dr. King asked the owner.

The police chief arrived at the restaurant. He arrested Dr. King, Rev. Ralph Abernathy, and 16 other people for being "unwanted guests."

After two days in jail Dr. King was released on bail. He immediately flew to Yale University, where he received an honorary degree. The Yale president predicted that "generations of Americans yet unborn will echo our admiration" for Dr. King.

But the problems in St. Augustine had not been solved. Dr. King returned to the city. Violence broke out again. Whites armed themselves with shotguns. So did Negroes. White youths blasted bullets into a Negro home. A Negro fired into a carload of whites.

Then a group of Negro and white demonstrators returned to the restaurant where Dr. King had been arrested. This time they wanted to swim in the pool at the adjoining motor lodge.

"This is private property," the owner said, "and I

will have to ask you to leave."

Two white men said the Negroes were their guests. They all jumped into the pool. Furious, the owner dumped two containers of acid into the pool. But the swim-in didn't end. The demonstrators realized there was enough water in the pool to dilute the acid. Policemen finally arrested the swimmers, including 16 Jewish rabbis.

The demonstrations continued. Negroes and whites returned to the ocean beaches. Governor Bryant, afraid that angry whites would attack the demonstrators, ordered state troopers to join the wade-in. The troopers, dressed in bathing suits, used police dogs to protect the demonstrators.

Dr. King announced that the city's businessmen had agreed to integrate their hotels and restaurants. White segregationists reacted by pressuring the businessmen. They forced the businessmen to back out of the agreement.

Then Congress approved the Civil Rights Act of 1964. An agreement between Negro leaders and St. Augustine's businessmen was no longer necessary. The new law required businessmen to take down their Whites Only signs.

Dr. King and a group of Negro leaders were invited to the White House on July 2 to watch President Johnson sign the bill into law. The new law, President Johnson said, "does not give special treatment to any citizen." It does, however, say that "those who are equal before God shall now also be equal in the polling booths, in the classrooms, in the factories, and in hotels and restaurants and movie theatres, and other places that provide service to the public."

It was a big step forward. But to the average Negro in a Northern city ghetto that summer, the new law didn't seem to touch his life directly. He still lived in a hot, overcrowded, often overpriced tenement. He still had to listen to rats chewing their way through his apartment at night. He still couldn't get a job. He felt trapped. And he began to listen to the black racists and their gospel of violence.

Like a pile of oil-soaked rags in a hot, stuffy cellar,

the ghettos exploded into flames during the summer of 1964. Harlem, Jersey City, Philadelphia, Rochester all felt the racking pains of rioting.

The violence worried Dr. King. Immediately, he asked the ghetto residents to resist the temptation to riot. "Lawlessness, looting, and violence cannot be condoned whether used by the racists or the reckless of any color," he said.

Some think the rioting might have been worse that summer without Dr. King's influence. He spoke to the people. Violence, he said, was not the solution to the Negroes' problems. Most ghetto residents listened to him.

The conditions that caused the riots, he realized, would not go away by themselves. Dr. King warned, "Until the Harlems and racial ghettos of our nation are destroyed and the Negro is brought into the mainstream of American life, our beloved nation will be on the verge of being plunged into the abyss of social disruption."

The time had come, he decided, to move the civil rights struggle into politics. The nation would elect a President in the fall of 1964, and Dr. King knew the Negro vote could be an important factor. He gave strong support to the Mississippi Project—a campaign to register the state's Negroes as voters. Thousands of Negro residents there had never voted.

Three young volunteers—two whites and a Negro—were murdered by white racists for participating in the project. If the murderers intended to kill the project, their intent backfired. Hundreds of civil rights workers poured into the state, determined to register voters. The project was a huge success.

Dr. King moved directly and personally into politics. For the first time, he decided to support a candidate publicly.

Senator Barry Goldwater, the Republican presidential candidate, disturbed Dr. King. The Senator had voted against the civil rights bill. And Dr. King feared that much of the senator's support came from people who opposed the Negro drive for equality. So Dr. King campaigned hard for the election of President Johnson. He traveled through the North and South, urging people to vote for Mr. Johnson.

In September the mayor of West Berlin invited Dr. King to come to West Germany to speak at a concert honoring the memory of President Kennedy. While he was in Europe, Dr. King traveled to Rome for an audience with Pope Paul VI. The two men discussed civil rights and religious problems. After his visit with the Pope, Dr. King told reporters, "He said he was a friend of the Negro people and that he is following our struggle in the U.S." Dr. King said he was pleased to learn that the Pope planned to speak out against racial injustice.

Encouraged by his reception in Berlin and Rome, Dr. King returned to Atlanta. The past weeks and months had been crammed with activity—demonstrations, arrests, speeches, more demonstrations. He was tired. So, hoping to get a little rest, he checked into an Atlanta hospital for a checkup.

He didn't get much rest. Just before 9 a.m. on October 14, Mrs. King called her husband at the hospital. She had just heard the news bulletin on the radio. He had won the Nobel Peace Prize. "I thought I was still asleep," he said later. "I thought I was dreaming."

Word flashed around the world. Reporters and photographers swarmed to the hospital for interviews and pictures. Friends and people who didn't know Dr. King personally telegrammed their congratulations. Most people echoed the thoughts of United Nations official Dr. Ralph Bunche, the only other American Negro to win the Prize.

"This announcement by the Nobel Peace Prize Committee," Dr. Bunche said, "is a striking international recognition of the cause and struggle of the American Negro for full equality in the American society and for full participation in the mainstream of American life."

Not everyone congratulated Dr. King. Some people bitterly criticized the Committee's decision. "They don't know him," Bull Connor said. "They're scraping the bottom of the barrel when they pick him. He's caused more strife and trouble in this country than anyone I can think of."

A few weeks before Dr. King received the award in Oslo, Norway, controversy over Dr. King grew more heated. J. Edgar Hoover, Director of the Federal Bureau of Investigation, called Dr. King "the most notorious liar in the country."

Mr. Hoover was angry because Dr. King had criticized the FBI for not finding the killers of the three civil rights workers in Mississippi and the Sunday school children in Birmingham. Mr. Hoover's remarks made front-page headlines all across the country.

Dr. King responded quietly. "I cannot conceive of Mr. Hoover making a statement like this without being under extreme pressure. . . . Therefore I cannot engage in a public debate with him. I have nothing but sympathy for this man who has served his country so well."

Dr. King met with Mr. Hoover in Washington, D.C., on December 1. Dr. King left satisfied. The FBI Director had promised that there would soon be some arrests in the Mississippi murders. Three days later 21 persons, including a county sheriff, were arrested.

In Norway, it was easy for Dr. King and his wife to forget the controversy at home. Hundreds of cheering Norwegians ignored the chilling rain to greet the Kings at the Oslo airport.

The Kings had not traveled alone. They shared this moment of triumph with 26 relatives, friends, and staff members. The travelers had taken money out of savings accounts and borrowed in order to make the trip. "We are all of us very poor people," one of them said.

The largest crowd ever to witness the Nobel Prize ceremonies jammed the Oslo University auditorium on that Thursday morning. Before the awards were presented, the Norwegian Broadcasting Orchestra played a medley of songs from *Porgy and Bess,* the American musical about a poor, crippled Negro and the woman he loves. The music affected Dr. King, who dried his tear-filled eyes several times.

Then herald trumpets blared. Dr. King marched forward to receive his award. The man who so many times had marched in America's streets, dressed in a laborer's clothes, smiled as he moved forward. That morning he wore formal clothes.

Gunnar Jahn, Chairman of the Peace Prize Committee, presented Dr. King with his medal and scroll. Mr. Jahn praised Dr. King as the first Negro leader in America or Europe to show that racial discrimination can be fought without violence.

Then Dr. King spoke. For the first time he hinted publicly that he was about to expand his nonviolent movement outside the civil rights struggle.

"I conclude that this award," he said, "is profound recognition that nonviolence is the answer to the crucial political and moral question of our time—the need for man to overcome oppression and violence. . . . The tortuous road which has led from Montgomery, Alabama, to Oslo bears witness to this truth."

The thunder of applause interrupted the speech.

"I refuse to accept the cynical notion," he said, "that nation after nation must spiral down a militaristic stairway into the hall of thermonuclear destruction. I believe that unarmed truth and unconditional love will have the final word in reality."

He would no longer be known simply as a civil rights leader. Dr. King was now an international figure—a symbol of peace and nonviolence to people all over the world.

The next night Dr. King delivered the Nobel Lecture. Hundreds of torch-carrying students filled the square outside the auditorium where Dr. King was speaking. Huddled outside in the cold, the students listened to the applause of the enthusiastic audience inside. Closing his speech, Dr. King used a line from a Negro spiritual, "We shall be free at last."

Outside, the students chanted the words—"Free at last! We shall be free at last!" The flickering light from their torches mixed with the reflections from a huge, glimmering Christmas tree that lit up the square.

"We shall be free at last!" the students shouted.

In Oslo that night people shared a feeling of peace and hope.

In Atlanta, Dr. King's hometown, plans to honor the Nobel Prize winner were running into trouble. Some

Atlanta leaders sent letters to more than 100 of the city's influential citizens, urging them to help sponsor a banquet honoring Dr. King on January 27. Two weeks after the letters had been mailed, most people had not replied. A few refused to attend. Some strongly objected to the tribute.

Mayor Ivan Allen, Jr. gave strong support to the banquet plans. A small group quietly began to make behind-the-scenes phone calls to businessmen, educators, religious leaders, and politicians. Gradually the list of sponsors grew. When the plans were made public, tickets were sold so fast some requests had to be refused. The hotel where the banquet would be held could seat only 1,400 people. Hundreds more wanted to attend, but were turned away.

Mayor Allen spoke for the people of Atlanta at the banquet. "Under Dr. King's leadership," he said, "the philosophy of the nonviolent movement is being proved. His deep and complete dedication and devotion to this method of social revolution has won him recognition by the Nobel Committee.

"I take great pride," the Mayor said, "in honoring this citizen of Atlanta who is willing to turn the other cheek in his quest for full citizenship for all Americans."

In a dramatic show of their respect and admiration for Dr. King, the entire audience rose to its feet. More than half of the people at the banquet were white Southerners who had never sung the Negro freedom song before. But that night, black and white voices as one, they sang "We Shall Overcome." Dr. King was pleased by the tribute to him. But he made it clear that the struggle was not over.

"I must return to the valley," Dr. King said. "I must return to the valley all over the South and in the big cities of the North——a valley filled with millions of our white and Negro brothers who are smothering in an airtight cage of poverty in the midst of an affluent society."

In Selma, Ala., that very night, plans were being made for Dr. King's arrival—for his "return to the valley."

Chapter XII

Selma:
Dogs, Hoses,
And Voting Rights

The seat of Dallas County, Ala., Selma had a population of 29,000. With 15,000 Negroes and 14,000 whites, there was no question as to who was in the majority.

But white citizens were in firm control of the city. Only 350 Negroes were registered as voters. The remaining Negroes had no voice in Selma's affairs.

In the summer of 1964 Selma had been the scene of a bitter series of civil rights demonstrations. Hundreds of demonstrators were jailed and the city's image was badly scarred.

When Dr. King arrived in January 1965, most Selma citizens wanted to avoid trouble. They had learned two important facts about the nonviolent movement. Physical opposition to nonviolent protest makes the opponent look brutal. And brutality rallies sympathy and support for the protesters. That is what happened in Montgomery and Birmingham. Whites in Selma hoped it would not happen there.

Selma planned to turn the other cheek when the demonstrations began. If the city did not react to the demonstrations, Maj. Joe Smitherman hoped, Dr. King's campaign would fizzle and people would lose interest.

The city's Commissioner of Public Safety, Capt. J. Wilson Baker, stood quietly by as Dr. King checked into the Albert Hotel. It was the first time that a Negro guest had been admitted to the century-old hotel.

The sight of a Negro signing the hotel's guest register triggered a white man's anger. A white racist ran forward and threw two quick punches at Dr. King.

Captain Baker pushed his way through the lobby. He grabbed the white attacker and forced him out to a police car.

"We're simply trying to enforce the law in an impartial manner," Captain Baker said.

The Commissioner of Public Safety had let Negroes demonstrate within "the letter of the law" for several days. Although a few demonstrators were arrested for breaking local laws, the city police department did not interfere with most of the protests. And Selma policemen protected the demonstrators from angry whites.

The Negro demonstrations centered around the Dallas County Courthouse, where people registered as voters. County Sheriff James G. Clark, Jr. was responsible for keeping order at the courthouse.

Sheriff Clark bitterly disagreed with Captain Baker's methods. He ordered all Negroes who had gone to the courthouse to register as voters to wait in a side alley. When some refused, they were arrested for unlawful assembly. Sheriff Clark personally grabbed a woman leader of the group and pushed her into a patrol car.

Selma officials and businessmen were worried. They were afraid that Sheriff Clark would indirectly create a wave of sympathy for the demonstrators. They tried to convince him not to make unnecessary arrests. He refused to make any promises.

The next day Sheriff Clark saw Captain Baker standing near a group of Negroes who were waiting to register as voters. The two men didn't speak. Sheriff Clark sent an assistant to Captain Baker with an order to send the crowd home.

Instead, Captain Baker told the Negroes that if they formed an orderly line they would be able to use the courthouse door that Sheriff Clark had forbidden them to use.

Quickly and quietly, they formed the line. Sheriff Clark watched in shocked disbelief. Then he moved to the front of the line and gave the Negroes one minute to leave the area. They stayed. Sheriff Clark arrested more than 100.

It was growing obvious to Dr. King's staff that Selma's official plan to ignore the demonstrations might not work. One staff member smiled and said, "Jim Clark is another Bull Connor. We should put him on the staff."

Until February 1 all of the Negro marches to the county courthouse had been made by fewer than 20 people at a time. A larger group would have been required by Selma law to obtain a parade permit.

Then Dr. King decided to lead a larger group of marchers to the courthouse. About 260 people met outside Browns Chapel Methodist Church on a cold, drizzly day. Dr. King told them to march together as a single group. They had walked for about three blocks when Captain Baker stopped them.

"This is a deliberate attempt to violate the city's parade ordinance," he said. "You will have to break up into small groups."

"We don't feel that we're disobeying any law," Dr. King replied. "We feel that we have a constitutional right to walk down to the courthouse."

The marchers moved forward for two more blocks. Then Captain Baker stopped them again. "Each and every one of you," he said, "is under arrest for parading without a permit."

While Dr. King and the other marchers were being taken to jail, more than 500 Negro schoolchildren were picketing the courthouse. Sheriff Clark reminded the students that they were not allowed to demonstrate while court was in session. He ordered them to leave.

The students answered with a verse from a civil rights song, "Ain't Gonna Let Nobody Turn Me 'Round." Several hundred students were arrested that afternoon.

Selma had failed in its attempt not to react. The police had enforced a local law strictly and Dr. King, the Nobel Prize winner, had been arrested. The story made worldwide headlines. Dr. King knew the publicity would help the voting rights campaign, so he refused to be bailed out of jail for five days.

While he was in jail he wrote, "When the King of Norway participated in awarding the Nobel Peace Prize to me he surely did not think that in less than 60 days I would be in jail. . . . Why are we in jail? . . . This is Selma, Alabama. There are more Negroes in jail with me than there are on the voting rolls."

Dr. King was released from jail on February 5. The

marches continued and more people were arrested. The police were not violent. They did not hurt the marchers, but they continued to enforce the local law.

The publicity over Dr. King's arrest faded into the background. Interest in the Selma campaign slacked off as the nation turned its attention elsewhere. It began to look as though the city officials' plan might work after all.

Dr. King's staff sensed what was happening. "Selma, a brutal city in the past, suddenly has become calm," a staff member told the press. "Actually, this is just a sophisticated source of oppression. They put on a nice polite image but keep you enslaved."

A group of segregationists in Marion, Ala., pushed the campaign back into the headlines on February 18. The town, located 30 miles from Selma, was the scene of a civil rights march that night. A white mob and some state troopers moved in to stop the march.

A shot was fired and a 26-year-old Negro, Jimmie Lee Jackson, dropped to the ground, clutching his bleeding stomach. A state trooper, Jackson said, had shot him. Eight days later, Jimmie Lee Jackson died.

Dr. King spoke to the 4,000 Negroes at Jackson's funeral on March 3. "His death says to us that we must work passionately and unrelentingly to make the American dream a reality."

As the next step, Dr. King proposed a protest march from Selma to Montgomery, the state capital. He knew there would be bitter opposition to the march. "I can't promise you," he told his followers, "that it won't get you beaten."

Alabama Gov. George Wallace ordered state troopers to take "whatever steps are necessary" to stop the march. The march, he said, was a threat to public peace and safety. But the marchers refused to give up their plan.

A cold wind chilled the 525 marchers as they met at the Browns Chapel Methodist Church on that Sunday afternoon, March 7th. They had come prepared to walk the 54 miles between Selma and Montgomery. With bedrolls and blankets, packs and paper sacks, they were ready to march.

They set out, two by two. They were quiet. It was going to be a long, difficult march and they thought about the road that lay ahead. They marched the six blocks to Broad Street without any trouble. Then they turned toward Pettus Bridge, the bridge that would take them out of Selma to the highway that led to Montgomery.

As they approached the bridge, they passed a small group of armed men—volunteer members of a posse organized by Sheriff Clark. The long line of marchers passed by quietly.

But at the other end of the bridge the highway was blocked. Blue-uniformed state troopers stood shoulder to shoulder across the four lanes of U.S. Highway 80. As the marchers moved forward, more slowly now, the troopers pulled on gas masks and held their nightsticks high. Behind them stood more members of the posse, including a dozen on horseback.

The Negro marchers edged forward until they were 50 feet from the troopers.

"Halt."

The marchers stopped.

"This is Major John Cloud," said the voice coming over the portable amplifying system. "This is an unlawful assembly. Your march is not conducive to public safety. You are ordered to disperse and go back to your church or to your homes."

One of the Negro leaders of the march asked, "May we have a word with the Major?"

The answer came back quickly. "There is no word to be had."

The two men exchanged the same words two more times. Then the Major said, "You have two minutes to turn around and go back to your church."

The marchers did not move. They stood motionless, in tense silence. Then came the order: "Troopers, advance!"

The line of troopers uncoiled like a spring squeezed under pressure and suddenly released. They charged, swinging their nightsticks. The marchers' front ranks toppled under the rush. Packs and lunch baskets spilled across the highway. Those farther back tried to run away, then huddled together as the mounted posse charged them. Tear gas shells plopped into the crowd, covering the scene with a cloud of gray smoke. Most of the Negro marchers ran, coughing and crying.

Weeping, a Negro woman screamed, "Please, no! God, we're being killed." Across the street a group of whites cheered the troopers with the enthusiasm of fans at a football game.

A Negro woman, clubbed into half-consciousness, lay at the side of the road. A trooper, seeing her there, dropped a tear gas grenade beside her.

The posse chased the frightened marchers back towards the Browns Chapel Methodist Church. Near the church some of the marchers again tried to resist. They threw bricks and bottles at Sheriff Clark and his posse.

Captain Baker moved in between the two clashing groups. He held off Sheriff Clark and the posse while he persuaded the marchers to go into the church. More than 60 marchers were treated for injuries in an emergency infirmary set up in the parsonage next to the church. Seventeen marchers, with injuries ranging from broken ribs to fractured skulls, were taken to the hospital.

"Bloody Sunday," as many newspapers referred to the Selma violence, outraged the nation. Pictures of troopers beating unarmed men and women shocked America. Powerful support rallied to the Selma civil rights struggle.

The next day Dr. King called for a new march to Montgomery on Tuesday. He asked American clergymen, black and white, to go to Selma and join the march. The response surprised even Dr. King. More than 400 priests, ministers, and rabbis came to Selma—ready to march.

President Johnson worried that a new march would bring even worse violence. Dr. King worried, too. But he also feared what might happen if there were no march. Frustrated Negroes might have rejected his nonviolent message and started rioting. "I felt if I had not done it," Dr. King later explained, "pent-up emotions could have developed into an uncontrollable situation. . . ."

Then Dr. King learned that a federal court had forbidden the march for the time being. Dr. King had asked the court to guarantee protection for the marchers against the troopers and posse. The court replied that it needed time to make a decision and ordered Dr. King to postpone the march.

Before the court banned the march, President Johnson sent former Florida Gov. LeRoy Collins to Selma to try to keep peace. The court order made Collins' job easier. He met with Sheriff Clark and suggested that the Negroes be allowed to march to the bridge, kneel in the highway to pray, and return home. That would not violate the court order because the marchers would not leave the Selma city limits.

Sheriff Clark, who had been sharply criticized by many moderate Alabama citizens, agreed to the plan. So did Dr. King. The compromise march was on.

Dr. King led 1,500 marchers out onto the bridge. A line of troopers, just as on Bloody Sunday, blocked the highway ahead of the marchers. Just as before, the state police major ordered the marchers to retreat. But this time he said, "You can have your prayer and then return to church if you so desire." Quietly, the marchers dropped to their knees on the pavement. The clergymen led the marchers in prayer for 15 minutes.

As the marchers finished their prayers and prepared to return to the church, the state police major made a surprising move. "Troopers, withdraw!" he shouted. The line of men dissolved to the side of the highway. The road to Montgomery was open, inviting the marchers to move forward, tempting them to disobey the court order.

But Dr. King refused to be led into a trap. "Let's return to church," he said, "and complete our fight in the courts." Some of the marchers disagreed with his decision. They wanted to go on to Montgomery. But every one of the marchers followed Dr. King back to the church.

Many people in Selma breathed easier. Dr. King had led the marchers to the bridge and back to the church without any violence. Maybe, they hoped, the Selma demonstrations would end now. Within a matter of hours those hopes lay smashed on a Selma sidewalk.

Rev. James J. Reeb, 38, a white Unitarian minister from Boston, had gone to Selma to march with Dr. King. He and two fellow white ministers ate supper that night in a Negro restaurant. As they were walking away from the restaurant, they heard four or five white men yelling at them. "Hey, niggers," the group shouted.

The three ministers ignored the white men. Then the men ran towards the ministers, shouting, "Hey there, niggers!" One of the men carried a wooden club, about the size of a baseball bat. He swung at Reverend Reeb. "It struck Reeb in the back of the head with a sickening thud," one of the ministers said later. Reeb's body slumped to the ground and the white men attacked the other two ministers. They screamed at the other clergymen, "You want to know what it's like to be a real nigger?" The attackers beat the two ministers, and then ran away.

Reverend Reeb, his skull crushed by the savage blow, was taken to a hospital. Angry black and white demonstrators moved into the streets as soon as they heard about the beating. They sat down in the street, praying for Reverend Reeb's recovery.

Their vigil lasted around the clock, even during a chilling rain. Then Captain Baker told the demonstrators that Reverend Reeb was dead.

A shock wave swept out from Selma. All across America, people marched in sympathy to the Negro cause. Students even staged a sit-in inside the White House. They demanded that the Government step into the Selma struggle.

The following Monday night, President Johnson spoke before a joint session of Congress. "I speak tonight for the dignity of man and the destiny of democracy," the President told Congress and millions of television viewers.

"At times," he continued, "history and fate meet at a single time in a single place to shape a turning point in man's unending search for freedom.

"So it was at Lexington and Concord. So it was a century ago at Appomattox. So it was last week in Selma, Alabama. ... ."

The President promised to prepare a bill that would guarantee voting rights for all citizens. The Negroes' cause, President Johnson said, "must be our cause too, because it's not just Negroes, but really it's all of us who must overcome the crippling legacy of bigotry and injustice."

The President's Southern accent added a dramatic touch to his final words: "And we shall overcome."

A White House official told reporters later that the voting bill would be "simple, and it will work automatically. If a state won't register an American citizen, then the Federal Government will. We'll get them registered, and we'll get them voted, too."

There was little doubt that Congress would pass the voting rights bill. America demanded it. In Detroit, Chicago, Los Angeles, Boston and scores of other cities people protested the brutality in Selma. Public prayers for Selma were said in dozens of small towns and big cities. Religious leaders surprised many church members by speaking out on a public issue as they had never done before.

The day after President Johnson's speech to Congress about 600 Negro and white demonstrators in Montgomery began a march toward the city's courthouse. Montgomery policemen blocked their path a few blocks away from the courthouse, so the demonstrators sat in the street. They clapped their hands and sang freedom songs. "Freedom Now!" they shouted. "We shall not be moved!"

A dozen state troopers and deputies on horseback appeared at the end of the street. Slowly, the policemen rode towards the demonstrators, swinging clubs and ropes. A few deputies walked alongside the horses. They moved into the middle of the group of demonstrators—and a deputy sheriff swung his club at a young white man. The clubs swung back and forth, cracking heads and bruising bodies. The demonstrators got up and ran down the street, bleeding and crying out in pain and anger.

Dr. King went to Montgomery that night to calm the young demonstrators, most of whom belonged to the fiery and impatient Student Nonviolent Coordinating Committee. More than 1,500 people, ready to face police clubs or jail, listened to Dr. King. They would march for freedom again, he told them. On the next day he would lead them to the Montgomery County Courthouse.

They followed him, in a gentle rain. A police escort accompanied the march—and there was no trouble. Sheriff Mac Sim Butler, who had been with the mounted policemen on the day before, apologized to Dr. King for the brutal beatings.

Dr. King, standing on the courthouse steps, spoke to the 2,000 demonstrators through a megaphone. He had good news. A federal judge had just ruled, Dr. King told the crowd, "that we have a legal and constitutional right to march from Selma to Montgomery." The crowd's cheers drowned out Dr. King's voice.

The plan, as approved by the judge, called for a five-day march. Every step of the route was set down in detail. On the first day the marchers would travel 11 miles. Then 11 more miles the second day, 17 miles on the third, eight miles on the fourth, and the remaining four miles on the fifth day. Along the way, the marchers would sleep in tents in roadside campsites.

Governor Wallace knew it would not be easy to protect the marchers as they traveled and slept along U.S. Highway 80. He asked for federal help, although President Johnson suggested that the Alabama National Guard be called up to protect the marchers. The state, Governor Wallace insisted, couldn't afford to pay the National Guard. So President Johnson federalized the Alabama Guardsmen and ordered Regular Army units to stand by.

"Over the next several days, the eyes of the nation will be upon Alabama," the President told a news conference, "and the eyes of the world will be upon America. It is my prayer—a prayer in which I hope all America will join me earnestly today—that the march . . . may proceed in a manner honoring our heritage and . . . all for which America stands."

As soon as the march plans were announced, thou-

sands of people from all over the nation set out for
Selma. Many of them were religious leaders—bishops,
ministers, rabbis, and even nuns. Most of them had
never taken part in a civil rights demonstration before,
but the Selma struggle had stirred their consciences.

"Actually," a white Episcopal priest from a small
Northern town explained, "the only Negroes I'd ever
seen were porters on a train. I don't think I've ever
been comfortable with a Negro. I think I will be now."

They went to Selma to march for equality. And while
they were there, a Negro Baptist minister was their
leader. "Whatever Martin wants," a Roman Catholic
priest said, "I will do."

The march began on a bright March 21 Sunday afternoon. Men, women, and children, rich and poor,
black and white—they all marched with Dr. King. Included in the 3,200 marchers who gathered in Selma
were Dr. Ralph Bunche, the Nobel Prize winner, and a
little Negro girl from Selma who said she was marching
"for freedom and justice and so the troopers can't hit
us no more." A white man with only one leg kept pace
on his crutches.

Before he led the marchers out of Selma, Dr. King
spoke to them from the Browns Chapel steps. "Because
of the system," he said, "we don't have much education, and some of us don't know how to make our
nouns and verbs agree. But thank God we have our
bodies, our feet, and our souls."

The marchers headed for the Pettus Bridge, where
some of them had been beaten two weeks before. This
time there were no troopers blocking the highway, and
armed troops marched alongside the group for protection.

Sheriff Jim Clark stood quietly on a sidewalk, wearing his answer to the Negroes' plea of "Freedom Now."
A large button on his lapel read: "NEVER."

As a safety precaution the court order had allowed
only 300 selected marchers to make the trip along a
stretch of two-lane highway outside of Selma. Most of
the marchers rode back to Selma on special trains at
the end of the first day. They were to rejoin later on.

Early Monday morning the 300 set out again. The blistering sun beat down on the marchers that day, and the next day the clouds opened up and poured rain on them.

All along the way white segregationists jeered them. "Yankee trash, go home," the whites shouted. "Filthy scum . . . sewer rats!" But to Negroes, the marchers were a living symbol of hope. One old Negro man with a cane joined the marchers for awhile. "I just wanted to walk one mile with y'all," he said. "I been called a boy long enough, don't you think?"

There was no trouble. Soldiers marched at the front and rear of the parade Low-flying helicopters searched for snipers. Demolition experts looked for booby traps.

On the fourth day the marchers reached a stretch of four-lane highway again. People were waiting to join them. By late afternoon, on the outskirts of Montgomery, 1,500 marchers moved down the highway. As they neared the city limits, rain began to fall. But their spirits were high and they sang "We Shall Overcome" as they moved into Montgomery.

Thousands of people flocked into Montgomery Thursday morning. That afternoon 25,000 marchers stepped off towards the state capitol.

Governor Wallace watched the marchers approach the capitol from inside the building. The Confederate and Alabama flags flapped in a muggy breeze above the capitol dome. "That's quite a crowd," the Governor said, as the marchers moved up Dexter Avenue.

Although the Governor had earlier agreed to talk to a group of marchers from Alabama, he changed his mind at the last minute. When the delegation asked to see him, a staff member said Governor Wallace was not in.

One by one, the nation's best-known civil rights leaders spoke to the crowd. "Freedom!" the crowd chanted, "Freedom Now!" Then it was Dr. King's turn to speak.

"Today," he said, "I want to say to the people of America and the nations of the world: we are not about to turn around. We are on the move now. Yes, we are on the move and no wave of racism can stop us. . . . We are on the move now . . . not even the marching of mighty armies can halt us."

But, Dr. King warned the crowd, "The road ahead is not altogether a smooth one. There are no broad highways to lead us easily and inevitably to quick solutions. We must keep going!"

After the cheers faded, the marchers began to leave. The soldiers began the trip back to their armories and bases. And, as night blackened the Alabama sky, volunteers began driving marchers back to Selma. One of those drivers was Mrs. Viola Liuzzo, a white woman from Michigan.

She had driven a carload of marchers to Selma and was on her way back to Montgomery to pick up another group. A 19-year-old Negro volunteer from Selma, Leroy Moton, was riding with her. Out on the lonely two-lane highway, a car drew up behind her and followed tight to her bumper. Then it dropped back a bit and speeded up, smashing into her car's rear end. The sudden impact almost forced her car off the road.

The driver soon tired of playing tag with Mrs. Liuzzo's car. He pulled out, followed by another car, to pass. As the cars rushed by, a blaze of gunfire spit into the Liuzzo car. Mrs. Liuzzo's body slumped to the seat. Her car went off the highway and ripped through a barbed-wire fence. Moton, uninjured, saw one of the cars circle around and head back down the highway. He dropped down on the seat, playing dead, while flashlights lit up the car for a look at the victims. The killers were satisfied. They drove away.

Moton ran down the highway towards Selma. Waving his arms, he tried to flag down a car for help. One driver tried to run him over. Finally a truck driver stopped and gave him a ride.

The FBI went to work immediately. All night long, FBI agents searched for the killers. The following afternoon they arrested four men, all members of the Ku Klux Klan.

President Johnson went on television to announce that the suspected killers had been arrested. Mrs. Liuzzo, the President said, was "murdered by the enemies of justice, who for decades have used the rope and the gun, the tar and the feathers to terrorize their neighbors. They struck by night . . . for their purposes cannot stand the light of day."

He announced a federal attack on the Klan, which he called a "hooded society of bigots." He promised legislation that would break up the Klan.

The Selma campaign was over. It had not solved all of the Negroes' problems, but it had given the civil rights movement a positive push. In the summer after Selma, on August 6, President Johnson signed the voting rights bill into law. In the next 10 days 20,000 Negroes registered to vote for the first time. It was a major step forward for America's Negro citizens. The Negro was making progress, just as Martin Luther King, Jr. had said he would.

"Walk together, children," Dr. King said, "and don't you get weary—and it will lead you to the promised land."

But a long, rough road lay ahead.

Chapter XIII

Power:
Black, White,
And Vietnam

Dr. King looked North.

The first part of his campaign had been aimed at giving the Southern Negro back his dignity by challenging the segregation laws. The law of the land now reinforced the Negro's right to vote, his right to drink from the same drinking fountain as a white man, and his right to eat at any lunch counter.

In the big cities of the North in the middle 1960's there were no segregation laws, but there were still chains on the Negro. He lived an age-old vicious cycle —poor education in an ill-equipped school, inability to find a decent job or any job at all, and a home in a slum. And he watched his children enter the same cycle.

If he managed somehow to get a good education and a good job, still the cycle had its hold on him, for finding decent housing in the ghetto was difficult. Most of the good housing was in the suburbs, and Negroes were usually not wanted there.

After the successes in Montgomery, Birmingham, and Selma, there was an urgency and an impatience in the ghetto. The message coming out of those Alabama cities was loud and clear, "You are as good as anyone else and don't you forget it." But who could feel much human dignity when he shared his home with rats and roaches, when a father couldn't find a decent job.

Watts, a Negro ghetto in Los Angeles, had heard the message from Alabama in the summer of 1965. A riot was the people's answer.

Touring Watts after the riot, Dr. King stopped to talk to a group of children.

"We won," said the children happily.

"How can you say you won, when 34 Negroes are dead, your community is destroyed, and whites are using the riots as an excuse for doing nothing?" asked Dr. King.

The children answered, "We won because we made them pay attention to us."

There had to be a better way to get attention. Non-violence had gotten attention in the South. It might work in the North. He had to try.

For his target city he picked Chicago. His objectives in the ghetto would be better jobs, housing, and schools. Out of Chicago's total population of 3.5 million, one million were Negroes. Of the 50 square miles in which 500,000 Negroes lived, nearly half of the dwellings were tumbledown buildings that often lacked adequate plumbing. The city was spending $266 per pupil per year in schools in Negro neighborhoods, compared with $366 per pupil in schools in white neighborhoods. One in four of the employable Negroes did not have jobs.

Dr. King planned to lead rent strikes, picket lines, boycotts of stores and products, and school boycotts.

His chief stumbling block would be the political machine of Mayor Richard Daley. Like any machine, it needed fuel. The fuel was votes. Stoke it up with votes for the Mayor and it turned out favors such as better garbage collection, improved streets, a job for a friend, or a playground. Mayor Daley had Negro assistants. Negroes continued to vote for Mayor Daley because they were sure his Negro assistants were looking after their interests. But somehow things did not change fast enough for those in the ghetto.

In January 1966 Dr. King came to Chicago. He moved into a faded brick apartment building in Chicago's North Lawndale section. Residents called it Slumsdale. His third floor walk-up apartment looked out on a street lined with pool halls, saloons, secondhand furniture stores, and storefront churches. When the landlord learned who his new tenant was, he had the apartment cleaned and painted.

Even before Dr. King arrived in Chicago, his aides were visiting the people in the ghettos and recruiting them to participate in protests.

They did not always get a friendly reception. There

was talk that the people were thinking of Mayor Daley's power over welfare checks and housing project leases. Or maybe they were thinking that the Negro in Chicago did not have a chance against the existing systems.

"I have never seen such hopelessness," said one of Dr. King's staff. "The Negroes of Chicago have a greater feeling of powerlessness than any I ever saw. We're used to working with people who want to be freed. The Chicago Negro is beaten down psychologically."

By working through the churches, Dr. King and his aides managed to build up some support. During the spring they worked to set up a program.

They organized Operation Breadbasket. Through a boycott of businesses in ghetto neighborhoods that did not hire Negroes, 900 jobs were produced for Negroes by the end of the year. Negroes also persuaded the merchants to sell products of Negro-owned businesses and to bank at Negro banks.

A dozen tenant unions were formed. The members refused to pay their rent if one member had a grievance. This tactic forced slum landlords to make their properties more livable.

In June a shooting in Mississippi brought Dr. King face to face with another problem that would complicate his work in Chicago. "Black Power."

Mr. James Meredith had been shot on the first day after starting a one-man freedom march through Mississippi. Mr. Meredith's name and face had special meaning to many in Mississippi. His registration at the University of Mississippi as the first Negro student, in 1962, had been a major triumph over bigotry. It had not been simple at first. The violence on the campus and in the nearby town of Oxford, Miss., had cost two persons their lives. For a time Mr. Meredith attended school accompanied by armed federal marshals. But he had managed to graduate from the university and to go on to law school in New York. Mr. Meredith's lonely march in 1966 was supposed to demonstrate that his life was now safe in his home state.

Dr. King was conducting a SCLC meeting when he

heard the news. He called Mr. Floyd McKissick, the President of CORE. The two men decided to go at once to the Memphis hospital where Mr. Meredith, who had not been seriously hurt, was being treated. While they were visiting, Mr. Stokely Carmichael, SNCC's President appeared at the hospital.

After consulting with Mr. Meredith, the three civil rights leaders decided to lead a march from the very spot where Mr. Meredith had been shot.

It was during this march that Dr. King began to get clues to the new feeling in CORE and SNCC.

"I'm not for that nonviolence stuff anymore," shouted one marcher.

"If one of those damned Mississippi crackers touches me, I'm gonna knock his block off," called another.

"This should be an all-black march. We don't need any more white phonies and liberals invading our movement. This is *our* march," said another marcher.

Later the marchers began to sing the civil rights marching song, "We Shall Overcome." Dr. King noticed that when they reached the stanza that speaks of "black and white together," some of the marchers did not sing the words.

When he asked them why they were not singing that verse, the reply was: "This is a new day; we don't sing those words anymore. In fact the title should be changed from 'We Shall Overcome' to 'We Shall Over-run.' "

A few nights later, during a speech to a mass meeting, Mr. Carmichael said to the crowd, "What we need is black power." At that point, marchers jumped up on the platform and shouted, "What do you want?" The crowd answered, "Black Power." "What do you want?" "Black Power." Soon the crowd was chanting, "Black Power, Black Power, Black Power."

Dr. King knew that the violence and black separatism he had heard expressed during the march had found a slogan.

Black Power. To Dr. King it seemed a cry of disappointment, born of despair. It rose from the belief that the Negro could not win. It was a call to stick together. It was a call to manhood, black manhood. But it was a slogan without hope, thought Dr. King. It was a slogan without a program.

Later Dr. King begged Mr. Carmichael to drop the slogan. The SNCC leader insisted that the slogan did not mean violence, it meant economic and social power. Mr. McKissick agreed.

"But Negroes cannot gain that kind of power unless white people help them; the slogan excludes them," said Dr. King. "Why not use the slogan 'black consciousness' or 'black equality.' These phrases would more accurately describe what we are all about. The words 'black' and 'power' together give the impression that we are talking about black domination rather than black equality."

Mr. Carmichael replied that Black Power had more force and appeal than the sayings Dr. King had suggested.

Dr. King could not make the other two men see the danger of the slogan. To him, it seethed with violence and hate of white Americans and he could never agree to that. He returned to Chicago, certain that the slogan would split the civil rights movement down the middle.

In July Dr. King saw this come true. At the CORE convention in Baltimore, Md., the hall resounded with the cries of "Black Power, Black Power." The keynote speaker was Mr. Carmichael. "This is not a movement being run by the liberal white establishment or by the Uncle Toms. What you have been doing all the time is letting them define how we are going to fight."

Later Mr. McKissick spoke to the convention. "Black Power means taking over the government in the South where the Negroes are the majority. The Negro is saying today that it's going to be your funeral and my trial if you don't stop messing with me." The convention passed a resolution that said that Negroes should isolate themselves and seize power wherever they could.

At the NAACP convention, the organization's President, Roy Wilkins, told the delegates, "Black Power can mean, in the end, black death. We of the NAACP will have none of this. We have fought it too long. It is the ranging of race against race on the basis of skin color. It is the father of hatred and the mother of violence. It is a reverse Mississippi, a reverse Hitler, a reverse Ku Klux Klan."

Several days later Dr. King and Mr. McKissick were on the same platform before a mass meeting in Chicago's Soldiers' Field. Said Dr. King "Our power is in our unity." He spoke to the crowd of the need for nonviolent resistance and the futility of violence. "Our power does not reside in the Molotov cocktails, rifles, knives, and bricks."

Mr. McKissick told the people that black power meant political power, economic power, and a new self-image for Negroes. Black power is not hatred or violence, he said.

Both Dr. King and Mr. McKissick urged the crowd to boycott businesses that did not hire Negroes. They urged Negroes to "decide to fill up the jails of Chicago to put an end to the slums." But their show of unity did not fool the crowd. The people sensed the violence implied in the cry Black Power. The slogan had divided Negroes in their drive for equality.

After the rally Dr. King led a three-mile march to City Hall. With a strip of adhesive tape he attached a 12-page list of demands to the door of City Hall. The demands touched all the bases leading to a "just and open" city—housing, education, jobs, and welfare.

The Mayor ignored the demands.

A few days later in a dreary slum near Roosevelt Road, someone opened the fire hydrants in an effort to get relief from the 95 degree heat. After the police came to turn the hydrants off, a Negro man turned the hydrants back on. When the police tried to arrest him, the man called for help from his friends. A five-day riot followed, complete with fire bombings and snipers.

Dr. King and other ministers walked the streets trying to get the rioters to stop. They saw the vengeful acts of some policemen. "You're only making these people angrier the way you're acting," said one minister to a policeman. "I don't care," said the officer. "Move out, do you hear?"

After the National Guard brought the city back to

order, Mayor Daley had sprinklers installed on the hydrants so that they could be used to cool the population on hot days. He installed a portable swimming pool in one ghetto area.

The Mayor also set up a committee to study ways and means to improve the relationship between the police and the people of Chicago. This was a partial victory for Dr. King. At the rally two days before, he had asked for a committee that would investigate specific charges of police brutality to citizens.

So far Dr. King had not made much progress in getting the Mayor to improve ghetto lives. But finally he found a way to dramatize the Northern Negro's plight to the nation. He led Negro marches into the White Only suburbs of Chicago.

The working-class white people, mostly the children of immigrants, were ready for the marchers. They had made it to the suburbs on their own. "Why do we have to have *them* shoved down our throats?" some asked.

The scene in those white Northern suburbs in the summer of 1966 was worse than any seen by Dr. King in any Southern city except St. Augustine, Fla. The Negro marchers were greeted by volleys of rocks, bottles, and firecrackers. Waving Confederate flags, they chanted, "Nigger, Nigger, Nigger." A man shouted "Wallace for God." A group of white teen-agers shouted, "Hate, Hate, Hate." A middle-aged woman carried a sign that showed a spear-carrying African savage with the caption, "Kiss me, I'm equal." A few boys waved Nazi flags.

At first the Chicago police did little to curb the white violence, but finally, using their clubs, they went after the rock-throwers. The whites began to shout "Don't vote for Democrats."

Mayor Daley sent offers to build a few more ghetto housing units and to open up a few more jobs for Negroes. But Dr. King was determined not to settle for crumbs. Open housing was what he wanted. He wanted Negroes to be able to live anywhere they wished in the city of Chicago and he wanted the right to do so enforced by law.

Dr. King announced that he intended to lead

marches into the suburb of Cicero. Cicero had been the home of gangster Al Capone. It had also become a symbol of Northern discrimination. In 1951 a Negro family had tried to live in Cicero. A mob had attacked the family, invaded their apartment, thrown their furniture out of the windows and burned it. No Negro had had the courage to move into Cicero after that.

The threat of a march into Cicero brought the Mayor to the conference table. With him were powerful men in Chicago's housing and banking businesses. The agreement they wrote was all that Dr. King hoped for. It promised not only open housing but also improvements in existing housing. But it depended on the honesty and goodwill of the men who agreed to it. Dr. King believed they were sincere. Other Negroes at the conference table did not.

Denouncing the agreement as just another line of promises, a CORE member led a group of marchers into Cicero. There was white resistance, but the police kept it under control. The marchers moved in and out without a clash with the whites. The march was a Black Power reaction and it would be a Black Power victory if the agreement were not honored. And it was not.

Six months later—two years later—Negro housing remained the hopeless problem it had always been. Black Power, Negro hopelessness, white hypocrisy, and the split in the civil rights movement had defeated most of Dr. King's efforts.

During the last few months of 1966 Dr. King continued to hope and to try. He had hoped that the Chicago campaign would attract national attention to the situation of the ghetto Negro. But in the late months of 1966 most national attention was directed toward the war in Vietnam.

Dr. King walked the streets of Chicago, urging nonviolence, but young Negroes would say, "What about Vietnam?" As he said later, "The President is asking me to keep my people nonviolent, and yet he drafts them, trains them to kill, and sends them off to Vietnam."

He had felt committed to take a stand against the war since he won the Nobel Peace Prize in 1964. Accepting the award seemed to him to be a pledge to work for international brotherhood, to urge nonviolence at an international level.

In March 1967 Dr. King actively joined the peace movement, and spoke out strongly against his nation's participation in the Vietnam war.

He led 5,000 peace demonstrators in a march to Chicago's coliseum. There he called on "all of those who love peace" to combine the efforts of the civil rights movement with the peace movement. He called the war "an inhumane power unleashed against defenseless people."

A week later at New York City's Riverside Church, Dr. King delivered a full statement of his view of the Vietnam war. "I make a plea to my beloved nation," he said. "I see the war as an enemy of the poor. The war is doing far more than devastating the hopes of the poor at home. We are sending black young men to guarantee liberties in Southeast Asia which they have not found in East Harlem. On TV we have watched Negro and white soldiers die together for a nation that has been unable to seat them together in the same schools. I speak for the poor of Vietnam whose country is being destroyed. I speak for the poor of America who are paying the double price of smashed hopes and death and corruption in Vietnam. I speak to the leaders of my country. We must stop the war. We are on the side of the wealthy and we are making a hell for the poor."

On a chilly April day he led 400,000 marchers to the United Nations plaza where he told the crowd that the war was crippling the civil rights movement. "I'll preach nonviolence with all my might, but I'm afraid it will fall on deaf ears," he said. In February of 1968 he led a group of silent marchers to Arlington National Cemetery in Washington to pray for the Vietnam dead.

His activity in the peace movement brought him both criticism and praise from fellow Americans.

Said the U.N.'s Dr. Ralph Bunche, "He is, after all, an active clergyman and naturally sensitive to moral issues. But he should realize that his anti-U.S.-in-Vietnam crusade is bound to alienate many friends of the civil rights movement."

Said a New York rabbi, "Religious leaders like Dr. King will never again ignore vital moral issues like violence, war, bigotry, poverty, and ignorance."

Freedom House, an organization founded to study U.S. foreign policy, criticized Dr. King for lending his name to Communists and "Hate-America" groups. They further charged that since Black Power had slowed his nonviolent efforts, he was seeking attention in another way.

Said a Providence newspaper editorial, "As a man of conscience, Dr. King is compelled to speak out against the wrong of the Vietnam war just as he has been compelled to stand against the wrong of racial injustice.

Said a *Washington Post* editorial, "Dr. King's Vietnam speech [Riverside Church] was not a responsible comment on the war but a reflection of his disappointment at the slow progress of civil rights and the war on poverty."

Said the NAACP, "Civil rights battles will have to be fought and won on their own merits, irrespective of the state of war or peace in the world."

A *New York Times* article pointed out that "While Dr. King is attacking the war, the already weak civil rights movement is growing weaker and the public is growing more disinterested." The article went on to point out that Dr. King had stated in the past year that he had found just the right goal for Negroes. That goal was an economic Bill of Rights, providing jobs or a guaranteed income for not only Negroes, but for all the poor.

In early 1968, Dr. King turned his attention to achieving the goal of economic equality. He began to plan a mass march on Washington by the poor. They would pitch tents and stay in the city until Congress granted them an economic Bill of Rights. It would be a last stand for nonviolence, he wrote in *Look* magazine. If the Washington march should fail, nonviolence in the civil rights movement would be defeated.

The proposed bill would represent a drastic change

in the country's welfare system. After his experience in Chicago, Dr. King had become convinced that there were not enough white men of conscience who had the power to put justice into the present system.

He began to work on the details for the march. He checked on available places to pitch tents. He started a money-raising campaign. In a small chartered plane he flew into small towns to recruit marchers. Nonviolence training sessions were set up for the marchers.

In the midst of his preparations for the Poor People's March, he got a long distance call from Memphis. The garbage workers of Memphis had been on strike for months. Now it looked as if there might be violence. Could he come to Memphis for a few days and calm down the demonstrators? He agreed to come.

A few days later, he took a plane to Memphis.

Epilogue

Martin Luther King, Jr. will march no more. There are those who are not sorry.

A man in Manchester, N.H., wrote that Dr. King was a troublemaker and anti-American. A Georgia schoolteacher was dismayed over the stir caused by Dr. King's death. "I want no more of your left-wing brainwashing in my classroom," she wrote to the publisher of a student periodical that had reported the incident.

But the marching continues, and with increased feeling. It is as if Dr. King's death did more to stir the conscience of his country than did his life. Dr. King's murder was followed closely by the brutal massacre of Senator Robert F. Kennedy. Shock waves of antiviolence reaction were felt through the United States.

The quiet millions that make up most of the nation's population started to find their voices. There were new demands for strict gun-control laws from Congress. The Secretary of Agriculture was asked to explain in detail why millions of Americans must literally starve in the richest, most productive nation the world has yet known.

And the cry for equality for the black man NOW was louder, clearer and more persistent than ever.

In a small New England town the week after Dr. King was buried, a white businessman was asked why he had no Negroes working for him. He replied that they were lazy and more interested in welfare than work. In the same town other white businessmen sought out Negro leaders and asked for help in finding Negro workers.

People were asking, "What can I do?" In many instances the answers came in the form of action, not words.

As Dr. King's work passed on for others to continue, violence—and not nonviolence—still stalked the land. As new leaders filled the spaces left by those torn from the March to Freedom, the end of the March was not yet in sight.